THE

FLYING MACHINE

in Gloucestershire

THE
FLYING
MACHINE
in *Gloucestershire*

DEREK N. JAMES

TEMPUS

First published 2003

Tempus Publishing Limited
The Mill, Brimscombe Port,
Stroud, Gloucestershire, GL5 2QG
www.tempus-publishing.com

British Library Cataloguing in Publication Data.
A catalogue record for this book is available from the British Library.

ISBN 0 7524 3113 7

Typesetting and origination by Tempus Publishing Limited.
Printed in Great Britain by Midway Colour Print, Wiltshire.

Contents

This 1931 woodcut shows Jean Pierre Blanchard and his balloon setting out on the first air voyage in America on 9 January 1793. His little black dog accompanied him. Walnut Street Prison yard, Philadelphia, was the departure point.

Preface

The author is very much aware that, in 1974, due to changes in the boundaries of certain UK counties, the southern part of Gloucestershire, which included Filton and Yate, disappeared into a fabricated place named Avon. In 1996, Avon vanished and its northern regions returned to a newly created unitary authority named South Gloucestershire. To provide continuity of this book's storyline, Filton and Yate's twenty-two-year absence from a region of England with Gloucestershire in its name has been carefully ignored with the hope that all aviation, geographic and local administrative purists will not mind too much.

Before we set out on this journey through time in Gloucestershire we shouldn't forget that fifteen-mile aerial journey in a hydrogen balloon by Jean Pierre Blanchard which took place on 9 January 1793 and which ended near Woodbury in the County of Gloucester. Before we get too excited about this revelation, it must be made clear that it was Gloucester County, New Jersey. For the record, this was the first aerial journey in America. It had begun in Philadelphia's Walnut Street Prison Yard, its high walls giving the balloon protection from the wind and those members of the public who had not bought tickets to enter the Yard! It was not until 110 years later, on 17 December 1903 at 10.35 a.m., at Kill Devil Hills, Kitty Hawk, North Carolina, that Orville Wright, piloting the Wright *Flyer*, made the world's first manned, powered, sustained and controlled flight. It lasted ten seconds and covered 120ft. He was followed into the air by his brother, Wilbur, whose contributions made this flight possible. We now turn the calendar back to 1783 to record the story of The Flying Machine in Gloucestershire.

Acknowledgements

'No historical reference work such as this book can be prepared through the unaided efforts of the author alone. He is not required to make a single-handed voyage across the years.' I am sure that I have used these words before in another place, but they are equally relevant here. Without the help of many better-informed friends, colleagues and total strangers, not a key on my PC would have been prodded in pursuit of this story of aviation in Gloucestershire, which spans an amazing four centuries. I am, therefore, most grateful to Roy McCarthy at Dowty Propellers who began it all; to Michael Jones, Phil Collins, Rod Ashforth, Gary Murden, Allan Maycock, Jo Sadler and Duncan McGaw of Smiths Aerospace, and Tony Edwards, past President of the Royal Aeronautical Society and aviation enthusiast, all of whom gave me information, their time and much-needed support over a long period; to Peter Hall at Messier-Dowty and Duncan Greenman, guardian of Bristol Aeroplane Company's *Airchives* at Filton; Nick Stroud at *Aeroplane* magazine; Helen Tempest, Aerosuperbatics' brave and glamorous wing-walking exponent at Rendcomb; Bernard Smythe at Nympsfield and David Roberts, chairman of the British Gliding Association, at Aston Down; to Peter Watts of Retro Track and Air (UK) at Cam, Ted Currier of Gloucestershire Aviation Collection and Heather Johnson, HQ Bristol & Gloucestershire Wing, Air Training Corps; Anna Morris in the County Archaeology Dept; to my friends Jaqui Taylor at the County Planning Dept. and Jean Stanton in Berkeley; David Mullin of the Jenner Museum; to Mary Slinger of the City Library Local Studies Dept; Philip Moss, local historian; David Hanks of Cotswold Images; and fellow aviation authors Ray Williams, Malcolm Hall and the late Ken Wixey. As always my thanks go to my wife Brenda whose magic PC skills in un-dotting the 't's and un-crossing the 'i's have pulled yet another rabbit out of the hat for final grooming by Campbell McCutcheon, Wendy Tse and the team at Tempus Publishing, who I thank for their touching faith in me over many years.

Derek N. James
Barnwood, Gloucester,
December 2003

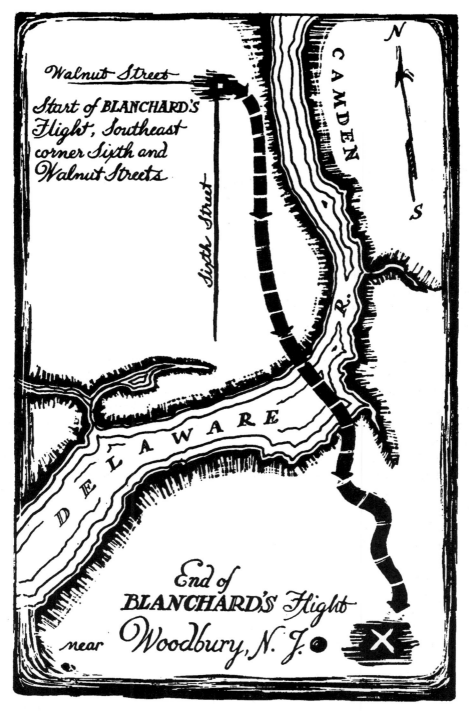

Blanchard's route crossed the Delaware River and he landed near Woodbury, County of Gloucester, New Jersey, having covered some fifteen miles in forty-five minutes.

one

In the Beginning

Apart from Berkeley's Jenner Museum, this splendid figure of Jenner stands in Gloucester Cathedral as a fitting reminder of this great man and all his achievements.

Almost any reference to the small town of Berkeley, some fifteen miles south of Gloucester, brings to mind two men named Edward. They are King Edward II, hideously murdered in Berkeley Castle in 1327, and Dr Edward Jenner, who first used vaccination to combat smallpox (the 'speckled monster' as he described this eighteenth-century horror affliction) and is known as 'the man who changed the world'.

In 1778 the twenty-nine-year-old Edward Jenner, a country doctor, naturalist and geologist, proposed to Catherine Kingscote but their marriage was forbidden because she was much younger than Jenner. They had to wait another ten years before they could marry. Thus, while pursuing a cure for smallpox he suffered bouts of 'melancholia'. However, in 1783 some news from France attracted his attention and helped to lift his spirits by providing yet another new field for research. Two brothers named Montgolfier had publicly demonstrated a small hot air balloon in Annonay on 4 June 1783. Two months later Jacques Charles released a hydrogen balloon from Champs-de-Mars, Paris. On landing, forty-five minutes later, it was destroyed by villagers who believed it to be a monster, the evil-smelling hydrogen which escaped adding to their belief. Then, at the end of that year, the first men to make a journey by air with a free balloon flight were François Pilâtre de Rozier and Marquis d'Arlandes.

The English newspapers' reports of these events inspired the scientist in Jenner to carry out his own experiments. With the support of the Earl of Berkeley, in around July 1784 he wrote to his friend Dr Caleb Hillier Parry in Bath, who had had some experience with balloons.

> Your directions respecting the Balloon are so clear and explicit, tis impossible for me to blunder; but to make it quite a certainty, I intend first to fill it & see if it will float in the Castle Hall, before the publick exhibition. Please to send me by return of Mr Marklove half a yard of such Silk as you think most fit for the purpose. I have got some oil ready.

When the balloon was made and coated with the 'oil' Jenner took it to the Great Hall of Berkeley Castle to inflate it with hydrogen, presumably made by immersing iron filings in sulphuric acid. On Thursday 2 September 1784 the balloon was taken to the Castle's Outer Court where it was inflated, a long celebratory poem written by a friend was attached to it, and at 2 p.m. Jenner released it. The balloon 'sailed over the hills' and landed at Symonds Hall about two miles northeast of Wotton-under-Edge, to complete a flight which was almost certainly longer than the six-mile straight-line distance between the two points. Indeed, a line from the poem forecast this: *Child of the Wind, I fluttered here and there.* From here records differ, one inferring that Jenner made a second balloon and demonstrated it to his beloved Catherine and the Kingscote family; others record that the first balloon was re-used. No further experiments with these aerostats by Jenner have been recorded and it is doubtful that he ever flew in a balloon.

Among the later brushes with aviation enjoyed by Gloucestershire during the eighteenth century was a flight from Stroud on 19 October 1785 by James Saddler who, a year earlier at Oxford, had become the first Englishman to fly in a balloon. It was in 1796 that an ale-house on Crickley Hill near Gloucester was named 'The Balloon'. Now 'The Air Balloon'

On 3 October 1838 John Hampton became the first Englishman to make a parachute descent. His balloon ascent from Montpellier Gardens, Cheltenham, parachute landing at Badgeworth and its design are clearly depicted.

In July 1910, Cheltenham Carnival witnessed, as its star attraction, the Willows II airship. Built in Cardiff, it was transported to Cheltenham's Montpellier Gardens and made a flight on 9 July. On the 11th, Willows decided to fly her back to Cardiff and set course for Dean's Close School. He circled and then flew off to Cardiff, where he landed safely. (Campbell McCutcheon)

a notice inside reads 'Many balloon ascents were made from around 1784 and one Walter Powell ascended from Malmesbury and disappeared without trace about that time. No evidence is recorded that he landed here.' In fact, Powell, Malmesbury's MP, after ascending from Bath, was blown out to sea at Bridport Bay, Dorset and was lost when his two colleagues leaped out of the basket when the grapnel, holding it down, broke free! A number of balloon landings were recorded in the south of the county but these were by flights launched in Bristol. Among these was a small unmanned balloon which, on 18 April 1785, arrived near the Cross Hands public house, Old Sodbury, frightening people in the vicinity.

On 3 August 1836 George Graham, accompanied by Mr Webbe, attempted an ascent from Cheltenham's Montpellier Gardens with his 18,000-cubic ft balloon inflated with coal-gas. Unfortunately, the gas was heavier than hydrogen and lacked its lifting power. Having dumped Mr Webbe, however, he was up, up and away for a fifty-five-mile flight to Oxford. Then, on 15 October, Graham got airborne with another balloon from Barrack Square in the City of Gloucester, near to the gasworks, which were at that time on the Quay. With him in the basket were two passengers; Mr Samuel Hitch, Resident Physician at the Gloucester County Asylum, and 'Mr William Pugh of this City'. This flight lasted twenty-five minutes, during which it is recorded that the balloon reached 12,000ft, and ended in a turnip field on Bredon Hill some sixteen miles away. The following year

B.C. Hucks in the Blackburn Mercury I, which he flew in Cheltenham and Gloucester during 1911.
(Malcolm Hall)

Mrs Graham followed her husband skywards from Montpellier Gardens; Charles Green also 'blasted off' from the same launch pad with his Royal Vauxhall Nassau Balloon. Then, on 18 September, John Hampton, a professional aeronaut, flew his Albion balloon from the Gardens. His big moment came on 3 October 1838. Though facing local opposition he planned a descent by parachute from the balloon. The umbrella-style parachute, which was folded, had a wicker basket for Hampton and was slung under the balloon. Gas to inflate his balloon was supplied on the understanding that it should be tethered. However, when the balloon reached 30ft Hampton severed the tethering rope and soared to 9,000ft. There he cut free the parachute which obligingly opened, taking thirteen minutes to descend. Landing at Badgeworth, three miles from Cheltenham, he became the first Englishman to make a successful parachute descent. These and other balloon ascents in the county laid the foundations for future interest and development of the aviation scene in Gloucestershire.

Around 1910-11 there were at least two attempts made to build and fly aeroplanes in Gloucester. At a site on the Quay two brothers named Scott at Webb Peet & Co., described as aeronautical engineers, designed and built a large two-seat canard-configured aircraft, its fore-plane acting as an elevator. The 40ft-span gull wing was very thin in section and, as lateral control was affected by wing-warping, its light structure enabled the trailing edge to flex. Two rudders were mounted well aft on the fuselage. Two tractor propellers, outrigged a short way from the fuselage, were chain-driven by a fuselage-mounted engine and a three-wheeled landing gear was used. A single 'steering rod' provided control in all three axes. It is recorded that the Phoenix Radial Rotary Motor Co. Ltd, whose Vulcan Works were in Quay Street, was producing these aircooled engines which the Scotts would have almost certainly intended for their aeroplane. Although Castle Meads, with the city council's permission, was earmarked as 'an aerodrome' there is no evidence that this aeroplane ever flew. A site in Barton Street also has been linked to a 1910 monoplane based on an early Blériot design.

In 1911 the county was visited by two pioneer aviators with their flimsy linen-covered aeroplanes. They were Sidney Pickles and Bentfield Hucks, this latter pilot having invented the engine-starting device which bears his name. They and their flying machines were a curtain-raiser on a new era of powered flight in Gloucestershire. By that time, Robert Blackburn in Leeds had built two types of aeroplanes and was launching another named Mercury I. In order to promote his products Blackburn arranged for Hucks to tour the West Country and South Wales in aid of charity, giving demonstration flights with this monoplane. A portable hangar was carried in a road vehicle which provided support for the

Three Royal Flying Corps pilots landed in Leckhampton to attend a Cheltenham wedding in 1913. Their aircraft from right are a BE.4, a Bleriot Xibis and a Henry Farman biplane.

tour. Having reached Cardiff and Newport, on 1 October 1911, at 6 a.m. he flew to Cheltenham. There the Mercury was exhibited in the Drill Hall, North Street, where it was a 'must-see' attraction for local people. Several flights took place from Whaddon Farm, Cemetery Road, until Hucks made a forced landing in someone's cabbage patch where a wheel came off and smashed the propeller. After repairs the Mercury departed to Gloucester on 16 October. Two days later, flying from The Oxlease bordering the River Severn on the city's western outskirts, Hucks caused a sensation by flying higher than the 225ft Cathedral tower. He then tried to improve on his personal height record but failed. It was at Gloucester that the Blackburn tour nearly came to an undignified end. On 21 October a gale lifted both the travel-weary aeroplane and its hangar completely clear off the ground; however, some rapid repair work enabled the last three scheduled flights to be made. An interesting feature of the Mercury I was that it was the first to be fitted with an engine revolution indicator which had been made by S. Smith & Sons. But more of Mr Smith later.

On 13 May 1912 the Royal Flying Corps and its Naval Wing were officially inaugurated. If not the first, then certainly a very early visit by military aeroplanes to Cheltenham came in October 1913 when three ex-Cheltenham College chaps, who were RFC pilots, landed their machines in Roland Field, Leckhampton to attend the wedding of one of their friends. Another young pilot 'borrowed' a DH.6 trainer, landed in a Cheltenham field and set off to visit a girlfriend; then forgot where he left his aeroplane! Earlier that year Sidney Pickles had returned to Gloucester flying from The Oxlease where he demonstrated his aeroplane. He then moved to a field at Hucclecote before going to Leckhampton on 27 March 1913 and giving a flying display there on each of the next three days.

But, despite the title of this book, Gloucestershire's aviation heritage isn't just about flying machines. The people of the county are vitally important to the story. In Cheltenham in 1885 a baby boy was born to Mr and Mrs Page and in 1892 Mr and Mrs Harris's baby was a boy. They grew up to become Sir Frederick Handley Page, the eponym who founded that great bomber-manufacturing company, and Marshal of the Royal Air Force, Sir Arthur Harris, whose gallant aircrews flew them during the Second World War. Clearly, these two aviation giants were destined from birth to succeed in life and become Knights of the Realm. Why? Page was born in Kings Road and Harris in Queens Parade!

In addition to the 'born-and-bred in Gloucestershire' men and women, the county seemed to be a magnet for others who moved in to establish new companies or additional production facilities. On 28 March 1854 Henry and Eliza White's fourth child was born in Cotham on the northernmost edge of Bristol. He was named George and, in 1904, was to become Sir George White Bt. Having launched the nation's first electrified tramway system in Bristol, in 1910 he went on to found an aircraft company at Filton in Gloucestershire. In Stoke Bishop, Bristol on 6 June 1885, Mary Elizabeth, wife of Henry Fedden, gave birth to a son whom they named Alfred Hubert Roy. Always known by the third of his Christian names, he became one of the greatest intuitive engineers in history, having joined George Whites' Filton Company in 1920. He was created a Knight in the 1942 New Year Honours List and formed his own company in 1943 at Stoke Orchard in the county.

A Bristol company which moved into Gloucestershire was George Parnall and Company, whose roots were in Parnall & Sons which, in 1820, had been established by Cornishman

William Parnall in the weights and measures business. In 1888 Henry Hubert Martyn founded H.H. Martyn & Co. in Sunningend, Cheltenham as a stone, marble and wood carving enterprise. It was in 1931 that young George Dowty from Pershore, Worcestershire, formed his little company in a Cheltenham Mews loft.

The relevance of these men and their companies to Gloucestershire Aviation may not yet be apparent, but they were to play major roles in its development. While they carved out their own particular niches in the county's aviation history, we must recognise and pay tribute to the tens of thousands of unnamed men and women who, with agile brains and dextrous hands created countless numbers of civil and military aeroplanes, aero-engines, systems and equipment. Nor must we forget the large numbers of them who lost their lives in enemy air attacks on their places of work or when test flying these aircraft. The Royal Flying Corps, renamed the Royal Air Force on 1 April 1918, was much in evidence in Gloucestershire with twenty-six airfields and eleven other Units. All these and the men and women who flew from them and worked at them, played an important role in two World Wars and in many campaigns over the years. We salute them all.

Undoubtedly, there were other, smaller, companies working in Gloucestershire Aviation but whose efforts and expertise have passed into history without record. Let this be a silent tribute to them too.

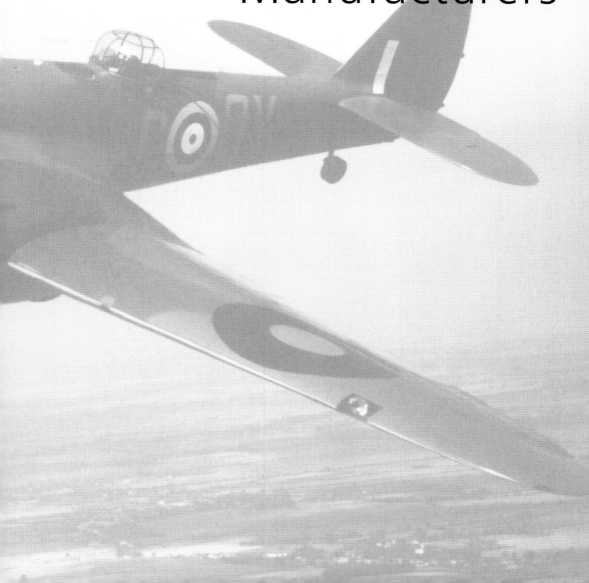

two

The Aircraft Manufacturers

Sir George Stanley White Bt, founder of the British & Colonial Aeroplane Co. in 1910 at Filton was described as 'a dapper Edwardian baronet, fierce in manner … a man to be reckoned with'.

As we have seen, aviation didn't miraculously arrive in the county overnight. It had to be created and nurtured. Gloucestershire is the only county to have had within its boundaries the main production facilities of four aircraft manufacturers, three aero-engine builders (a fourth having already closed) and what would become Europe's two largest major equipment and systems companies.

The British & Colonial Aeroplane Company

On 16 February 1910, Sir George White, in his role as chairman of Bristol Tramways & Carriage Co., told a shocked meeting of shareholders that he and his younger brother, Samuel, had been taking a close interest in the subject of aviation. During the previous year for health reasons he had visited France where he had seen a number of French aircraft, their designers and pilots. He was captivated by this new form of transport and had quickly obtained a licence to build the French Société Zodiac biplanes. He went on to say that he and his brother 'had determined personally to take the risks and expense of endeavour to develop the science from the spectacular and commercial or manufacturing point of view'. Cannily, he told them that a factory would be located on the tramway system and the flying demonstrations he had in mind would attract more passengers onto the trams. Although this family commitment to the still nascent business of aircraft manufacture appeared venturesome, there was no other way in which to provide the capital required. Members of the Bristol Stock Exchange, of which he was president, and local industrialists thought that White's declaration was sheer lunacy. Three days later he registered with the Board of Trade the names of four companies, eventually choosing 'The British & Colonial Aeroplane Co. Ltd' for his new venture which began trading with no less than £25,000 capital. In addition, it was all subscribed by Sir George, his son, brother and two nephews. This was in marked contrast with most of the other early aviation pioneers who lacked financial muscle. A few days later he gave instructions for some Bristol Tramways' corrugated iron sheds at Filton tram terminus in Gloucestershire to be cleared of production work on motor omnibus and commercial road vehicles and be prepared for leasing to the new British & Colonial Aeroplane Co. (BCAC) saying 'We're going to build aeroplanes here'. And build them they did; in Gloucestershire's first aircraft factory.

To kick-start production a French-built Zodiac biplane was sent to England with a written guarantee that it would fly. But it wouldn't. Its pilot's advice was to 'push it to the back of the hangar and forget it'. Sir George agreed, stopped five Zodiacs being built and wrote-off

Woodworkers busy building Boxkites in a very clean workshop at Filton in 1910.

Built for the 1964 film Those Magnificent Men in their Flying Machines, *the Shuttleworth Collection's replica Boxkite gets airborne.*

The company's first aeroplane with a 'tractor' engine installation rather than a 'pusher', the Racing Biplane was damaged beyond repair on its first attempted take-off in April 1911.

the whole exercise, putting it down to experience! However, he wrested 15,000 francs compensation from the Zodiac company for not supplying an aeroplane which could fly. With the collapse of the Zodiac programme the company studied the design of a Henry Farman biplane published in a magazine. Within days a set of drawings was made, and 20 aircraft were put into production. Three weeks later, on 19 July 1910, the first one flew. Initially named the Bristol Biplane it soon became known as the Boxkite.

But building aeroplanes was not enough for George White. He reasoned that a market for them had to be created; so he set up flying schools at Brooklands and at Larkhill on Salisbury Plain equipped with Boxkites. Flying at Larkhill attracted the attention of the Army and the War Office and soon Boxkites took part in manoeuvres on the Plain in the role of 'eyes-in-the-sky'. By the end of 1910 two French pilots had been employed, Boxkites had begun sales tours in Australia and India, and Filton was building two aircraft per week.

Boxkites were soon being surpassed by other companies' monoplanes but Sir George quickly responded. He invited British, French and Romanian engineers to join the Filton team to design monoplanes. When none of the military types won contracts the company built BE2, reconnaissance aircraft designed by the Royal Aircraft Factory at Farnborough. But things were to change with the outbreak of the First World War on 4 August 1914. Frank Barnwell had designed the Scout military single-seat biplane which had flown in the previous February and 367 were built, many serving with the RFC in France.

The first monoplane wholly-designed and built at Filton. Named the Bristol Monoplane, only two were built.

One of the last batch of thirty Scouts delivered during 1916. It was powered by a 100hp Gnome Monosoupape (single-valve) engine.

This BE.2c, No.1700, built by British & Colonial Aeroplane Co. is seen at Farnborough during the First World War. An airship shed behind it has been partially obliterated on the photograph.

A First World War vintage dual-control Bristol F.2B Fighter belonging to the Oxford University Air Squadron pictured in 1930.

Between 1915 and 1938 Barnwell was to produce a steady stream of designs, many as prototypes only, others in quantity. They began with a couple of military two seaters. Then came the renowned Bristol F.2B Fighter which was dubbed the 'Brisfit'. It was the RFC's most effective two-seat fighter once their pilots had worked out the best way to fly them in combat. Over 5,300 were built by BCAC at Filton and another factory at Brislington, and by eleven other manufacturers in the UK and USA.

Sadly, during the evening of 22 November 1916, Sir George White died aged sixty-two. A heavy smoker and a workaholic he had been in failing health for some time. Tragically, he died as he had lived, working hard at his desk.

The M.1 was BCAC's first military monoplane with production reaching 130 and which were flown by a small number of RFC squadrons in the Middle East. Then came the MR.7, almost a metal Bristol Fighter, two of which were made. A closer 'Brisfit' copy was the three-seat civil Tourer which had a production run of thirty-three. Four Scout variants and assorted F.2C and Badger two seaters were followed in 1918 by a small group of big four-engined triplanes. These were a couple of Braemar bombers, the fourteen-seat Pullman and two Tramps, the latter pair never getting off the ground.

The Braemar II triplane bomber had four 230hp Siddeley Puma engines in 'push-me-pull-you' pairs. It did not enter production.

When peace returned at 11 a.m. on 11 November 1918 the company soon focussed its attention on civil aircraft. First came three diminutive single-seater Babes in a bi-plane and monoplane configuration, then the Bullet which was a flying engine test-bed and a racer. They were followed in 1920 by the two-seat Seely built for an Air Ministry competition encouraging designs combining safety in the air with passenger comfort. Next was a pair of Ten Seaters with, not surprisingly, ten passenger seats and a Brandon ambulance/transport aircraft. The Bullet was to become an important element of a major event of BCAC history: its prime function was to test the Jupiter air-cooled radial engine made by Cosmos Engineering Co. of Fishponds, Bristol. Originally named Brazil Straker, in 1918 this company was taken over by the big Cosmos industrial conglomerate; sadly, in February 1920, it went 'belly-up' following a disastrous commercial gamble. Fortunately, Roy (later Sir Roy) Fedden, Cosmos' chief engineer and L.F.G. Butler, his assistant, kept the design team together working on Jupiter engines until a new owner could be found.

Meanwhile, on 23 March BCAC went into liquidation. Someone discovered that by closing BCAC and transferring its fixed assets to a new trading company – the Bristol Aeroplane Co. (BACo) – much less Excess Profit Tax would have to be paid. Thus, Bristol Aeroplane Co. acquired all British and Colonial's assets at a cost of about £300.

Although Fedden's engines impressed BACo's directors, it was only with continued Government pressure that they agreed to take over Cosmos. For £15,000 they got Fedden and Butler; thirty-one engineers; five Jupiter engines, with a promised order for ten more; and a load of tools, drawings and spares. They would form the nucleus of a new BACo aero-engine department at Filton.

Three Babes were built, one of them in a monoplane configuration. Test pilot Cyril Uwins in the cockpit prepares for its first flight in November 1919.

This refurbished M.1B Monoplane Scout was given a glossy scarlet coat in September 1920 and won a number of major air races.

The RAF Brandon ambulance aircraft was developed from the civil Ten Seater passenger aeroplane. The specially ventilated fuselage had a gloss white painted internal finish.

Barnwell's Jupiter-engined Bullfinch was an all-metal fighter monoplane convertible to a two-seat reconnaissance biplane. Two for the price of one – but it wasn't ordered. The Taxiplane and Primary Trainer Machines using the Bristol, *nee* Cosmos, three-cylinder Lucifer engine, won twenty-eight orders. Other Bristol-powered types were the 1922 Racer with its engine totally encased in its barrel-shaped fuselage, the Bloodhound two-seat fighter and the Jupiter Fighter and Advanced Trainer. They were a bunch of twenty-six aircraft which, photographically, all looked rather bewildered. In 1925 the Berkeley two-seat bomber temporarily broke the mould by having a Rolls-Royce Condor in-line engine, but failed to win orders. Fortunately, the aero-engine department didn't depend on Bristol aeroplanes to get its products airborne. Jupiters were being licence-built in France and were in service worldwide.

Soon the rattle of high-tensile steel strip being rolled into various shapes for airframe construction was being matched by the roar of Bristol engines on test. The Brownie, Boarhound, Beaver and Bagshot, the Bulldog and Bullpup plus Bristol Types 109, 110A, 118 and 120 all had metal airframes and Bristol engines. Only the Badminton racer and the Type 101 two-seat fighter had mainly wooden construction. All were biplanes except the little Brownie light aeroplane and the Bagshot twin-engined fighter. The company's last biplane, the Type 123 fighter, had cantilever wings with no external bracing and the dubious Rolls-Royce evaporatively-cooled Goshawk engine. Few of these aeroplanes got beyond the prototype stage. The Bulldog single-seat biplane fighter with Bristol's Jupiter or Mercury engines was the exception. Nearly 450 were built for the RAF and the Air Forces of eight other countries. When orders dried up BACo became a sub-contractor. In 1919-20 Filton built 168 Parnall Panther navy fighters, followed by 89 Armstrong Whitworth Siskin fighters.

Bristol's 1922 scarlet Racer was no lean mean machine because its radial engine was enclosed in the fuselage. The fragile-looking landing gear was retractable. This Racer flew six times and was then scrapped.

Three Brownie light aeroplanes were built for the September 1924 Light Aeroplane Competition at Lympne, Kent. Powered by Bristol Cherub 999cc two-cylinder engines they won two prizes.

Only one Bagshot twin-engined fighter was built in 1927. It would have carried two 20mm Coventry Ordnance Works cannon in RAF service. Note the aerofoil-section fairing on the landing gear axle.

The least known Bristol aircraft was the 1925 Type 92 Laboratory aeroplane used to compare wind-tunnel data with full-scale airborne data. It never flew out of sight of Filton and had no registration or serial number.

Bristol Bulldog IIA, K2227, as rebuilt, is seen flying in 1961.

It was May 1935 before the British Government forsook its policies of disarmament and appeasement and decided to strengthen and modernise the Royal Air Force. It was not a moment too soon. On 15 June Bristol Aeroplane Co. became a public limited liability company with a 4,200 strong workforce – most of it in the aero-engine business – and a 13-acre factory. Almost unknowingly, BACo was already preparing for war with a fast twin-engined civil transport, the Type 142 which was built especially to meet the requirements of Lord Rothermere, the owner of the *Daily Mail*. It first flew on 12 April 1935. On test at Martlesham Heath's Aeroplane and Armament Experimental Establishment its top speed was 50mph faster than the RAF's latest Gloster Gladiator fighters. Ultimately, this aeroplane was the basis for a light bomber design which became the Blenheim of which more than 5,500 were built. They flew with the RAF and with the air arms of Canada, Finland, Romania and Turkey. A Blenheim was the first RAF aircraft to fly over enemy territory on 3 September 1939, the first day of the Second World War.

At that time BACo was the world's largest single aircraft manufacturer with 2,700,000 sq ft of buildings. In October 1938 a new twin-engined torpedo-bomber had appeared in Bristol skies. Named Beaufort, with the Duke of Beaufort's permission, a total of 1,429 were built at Filton and Banwell and another 700 in Australia. Two months earlier Frank Barnwell had been killed in the crash of his own-design light aircraft. He was succeeded by Leslie Frise who had shared much of the design work since the Bulldog days.

A total of 445 Bulldog fighters were built. Here eight of them near completion for the Royal Australian Air Force in 1929.

This spatted Bristol Type 123 met Specification F.7/30 but problems with its almost-mandatory Rolls-Royce Goshawk evaporatively-cooled engine and incurable instability were unacceptable.

Bristol's second bite at the Specification F.7/30 was this Type 133 monoplane. It performed and handled well – until a pilot spun it with the landing gear down. He baled out, it crashed.

When fifty Bombay bomber/transports were ordered they were too big for the Filton hangars, so Short & Harland in Belfast built them. This was the first one.

Lord Rothermere's Bristol Type 142 high-speed transport aircraft which he bought, named it 'Britain First', and presented it to the nation. A military version became the Blenheim medium bomber.

This Bristol Type 138A high-altitude monoplane was used to probe the problems associated with stratospheric flight when the RAF anticipated aerial battles at ever-increasing altitudes.

This immaculately preserved Second World War Blenheim IV, serialled L8841, here carries No.254 Squadron code letters QY-C.

Dated 4 August 1937 this photograph shows Blenheim 1 bomber production at Filton. The overall cleanliness of the factory and the absence of people are noteworthy.

The burly Beaufort was RAF Coastal Command's standard torpedo/bomber from 1940 until 1943 when Beaufighters replaced it. This Beaufort carries No.217 Squadron markings.

The RAF's lack of a long-range cannon-armed fighter was met in 1939 by the Beaufighter. It carried cannon and machine guns with provision for a torpedo, rockets and bombs. With nose-mounted radar it was a highly effective night-fighter. It also entered production in time to save the company from having to build Short Stirling four-engined heavy bombers as a sub-contractor. Ultimately, 5,564 'Beaus' were built in the UK and 364 in Australia.

Meanwhile, enemy intelligence kept watch on Bristol's factories. Luftwaffe reconnaissance flights on 22 and 23 September 1940 revealed that No.501 Squadron's Hurricanes had left Filton to fight the Battle of Britain from RAF Kenley, Sussex. At 11.30 a.m. on Wednesday 25 September, a force of fifty-eight Heinkel 111 bombers with Messerschmitt 110 fighters struck. Over 100 tons of bombs fell on the factory site and surrounding areas. There were 281 casualties, 91 being killed when air raid shelters were hit. There were further attacks in subsequent years.

In February 1943 the first of another trio of twin-engined types flew. Too late to serve in the war this was the Buckingham light bomber. The Buckmaster trainer which flew ten months later was the second. It was used mainly to train crews for the third type, the Brigand light ground-attack bomber flown operationally in Malaya during 1950-54. Production of these three types totalled 382.

First of 5,900 Beaufighters produced, this prototype was photographed on 17 July 1939, the day it first flew. This prototype has a tailplane without dihedral.

On 12 June 1942 Flt Lt Ken Gatward and Flg Off George Fern flew a Beaufighter from RAF Thorney Island to Paris, dropped two Tricolour flags on the Champs Elysées and returned home, rarely flying above 100ft, often down to 30ft. They were never fired on. This is one of the many photographs George took en route to prove they had visited Paris!

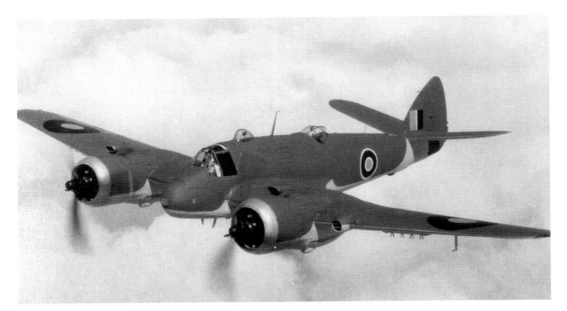

Above: *A Beaufighter
X. Royal Observer
Corps members described
the Beaufighter as 'Two
ruddy great engines
hotly pursued by an
airframe'.*

Right: *This photograph
was taken from one of
the fifty-eight Heinkel
111 bombers which
attacked the Filton
factories on
25 September 1940.*

No.84 Squadron Brigands in the Far East in 1951. When a propeller shed a blade and ripped the engine off the wing of the nearest aircraft, the crew baled out near Tengah, Singapore.

At the war's end cancellations of military contracts focussed BACo's management's thoughts on a search for alternative work for their employees. They identified several products: prefabricated houses and hospitals, high-quality cars and marine craft. Fortunately other help was at hand. The Brabazon Committee, named after its chairman Lord Brabazon of Tara who epitomised British aviation, had been formed in 1943 to consider the types of civil aircraft which Britain's airlines would need in peacetime. Five were recommended, the Brabazon Type I, a London–New York non-stop airliner, having priority. In March 1943 the Government announced that Bristol Aeroplane Co. had been given the job of creating this aeroplane. It was to be a long one. The design and engineering team were ready but a large new hangar was wanted. And what about the runway – was it long enough? The great 8-acre hangar was the easier bit. To extend the runway at Filton not only meant closing two roads but also knocking down part of the village of Charlton. A Cabinet decision was required before this destructive project could go ahead.

A Trans-Canada Airlines Wayfarer. Note the boxy square-section fuselage, bulbous nose, fixed landing gear and the lowered flaps.

While this 130-ton 230ft-wingspan monster, named the Brabazon, was being designed under the leadership of Leslie Frise, and built, BACo needed more immediate work. This materialised as a 'no-frills' twin-engined short-haul general-duty transport. Two versions were envisaged. The Freighter for cargo work, the Wayfarer for passengers. Pretty they weren't, but BACo sold 214 of them to operators in many parts of the world.

The Brabazon first flew on 4 September 1949, some 400 flying hours were logged and a second airframe was being built. Then, in 1952, the entire programme was stopped. And the bill? £6.3 million. Sadly, the Brabazon had turned out to be not only Britain's biggest aeroplane with wheels but also Gloucestershire's biggest white elephant. It was the source of many myths and stories. On the first take-off Bill Pegg who was the pilot, turned to

Outside its hangar the Brabazon begins engine-running checks. The 230ft span wings dwarf the ground engineers in attendance on the giant aeroplane.

Sunday 4 September 1949. Bill Pegg, Bristol's chief test pilot, gets the Brabazon airborne at Filton for the first time.

Walter Gibb in the second pilot's seat and said 'Well, my side's airborne, what's yours doing?' On landing he was asked what it was like to fly such a large aircraft. He replied 'Oh, we only flew the cockpit, the rest just trailed along behind'.

Back in 1947, although Bristol's Type 175 four-engined transport had not exactly met British Overseas Airways Corporations specification for a medium-range airliner for Empire routes, it was closer than seven other proposed designs. Thus, powered by four Bristol Proteus propeller-turbine engines and named Britannia, BOAC ordered it. The prototype first flew on 16 August 1952 in the hands of Bill Pegg. While its flight development programme was not without some white-knuckle moments, the Britannia won airline markets around the world, its purring Proteus engines earning it the name 'Whispering Giant'. But jet airliners were breathing down its elegant neck and only eighty-five were built.

BACo's move into rotary-winged aircraft came in 1944. Its first helicopter was the Type 171 single-rotor four/five seater which flew on 27 July 1947. The production of 178 of them was based at the company's Old Mixon factory at Weston-super-Mare. Named Sycamore, they flew with the RAF, were exported and a few went to civil operators. The second Bristol helicopter, the Type 173, had twin engines and rotors and thirteen seats. It first flew in January 1952. From it came the RAF's Belvedere, but only twenty-six were

In the Brabazon's shadow are from left: Bill Pegg, -?-, -?-, -?-, Dr A.E. Russell, chief designer (hands clasped), -?-, Sir Reginald Verdon-Smith, company chairman.

The first production Britannia 102, G-ANBA, seen in British Overseas Airways Corporation livery, was delivered in August 1958.

built. When deliveries began in March 1960 Bristol's Helicopter Department had become the Bristol Helicopter Division of Westland Aircraft; this resulted from the Government's decision to centre all British helicopter interests on Westland at Yeovil.

About five years earlier Bristol Aeroplane Co. had begun work on a supersonic transport project which became the Type 223 with four under-wing engines and a slender delta wing. Because of its similarity with France's Sud Aviation Super Caravelle, together they formed the basis of the Anglo-French agreement of 1962 which produced the Concorde.

Much to the relief of local inhabitants, no doubt, jet propulsion came late to Filton and it was not until 1946 that studies for a jet engine for long-range bombers began. But what a great engine it became! The superb Olympus. Under the almost magical influence of Dr Stanley (later Sir Stanley) Hooker who had joined the company from Rolls-Royce in 1949, Bristol's jet engine technology advanced at a great pace. The first wholly Bristol designed-and-built jet aircraft, the Type 188 research vehicle, did not fly until 14 April 1962. A part of the Concorde research programme, it was of stainless steel construction and

The Bristol Sycamore demonstrator helicopter flies near the Severn Estuary's mud flats. It served in the Royal Australian Navy before ending up crop-spraying.

XG452 was the fifth of twenty-six Belvederes built. Lengthy trials with different tail units produced the compound anhedral tailplane of the production helicopter.

Godfrey Auty, Bristol's chief test pilot, banks the T.188, serialled XF923, showing the wings and tail-unit shapes, and engine nacelles almost as big as the fuselage.

was designed to investigate kinetic heating of the airframe structure during sustained flight at twice sonic speed. The sole Type 188 appeared in the 1962 Farnborough Air Display where the public voted it the aeroplane with the highest 'Wow factor' and the Empire Test Pilots School students voted Godfrey Auty, its pilot, 'the man most likely to eject in 1963'! But its engines gulped fuel so rapidly that the T.188's flight time at full speed was too short to be of much value.

The second jet aircraft to have a BACo Type number was the Type 221 which, in fact, was the modified Fairey FD.2 which had set a world speed record at 1,132mph. It was used to probe the high-speed handling characteristics of an ogee wing shape similar to that of Concorde. Other research, development and production programmes produced the Bloodhound ground-to-air missile, the Red Rapier expendable bomber which was abandoned in 1953 and a number of space satellites and systems.

While the first Concorde prototype, 001, was assembled at Toulouse and flown on 2 March 1969, the Filton-built second prototype, 002, first got airborne on 9 April flown by Brian Trubshaw. Nine more Concordes were assembled at Filton using British and French components with a similar number being assembled at Toulouse. Britain's Concordes were test flown at RAF Fairford in Gloucestershire.

As part of the Government's rationalisation plans for Britain's aircraft industry, British Aircraft Corporation was formed in June 1960. This pooled Bristol Aeroplane's aviation interests with those of Vickers Ltd, the English Electric Co. and Hunting Aircraft. Three and a half years later they merged into a single unit, British Aircraft Corporation (Operating) Ltd of which Bristol became the Filton Division. In 1977 all but two of Britain's major aircraft companies merged to form British Aerospace and in January 1978 the Filton site became British Aerospace – Civil Aircraft Division. Then, in 1999, the name changed to British Aerospace Airbus Ltd when the company had responsibility for design,

Concorde 002 takes shape in Filton's assembly hall with the second aircraft, 001, beyond it.

development and production of wings for the Airbus series of aircraft. Later 'British Aerospace' disappeared and was replaced by BAE Systems, then BAE Systems Airbus UK in April 2000. At the time of writing the Filton site operates under the name Airbus UK.

The story of Bristol Aeroplane Co.'s Aero-Engine Department appears on pages 100-105.

Registered G-BSST, Concorde 002 takes off from Filton on 9 April 1969, urged on by its four Olympus 593 engines. Flight testing took place at RAF Fairford in Gloucestershire.

A British Airways 100-seat Concorde gets airborne. Note the small 'tailwheels' visible below the starboard engines.

Above: *The first set of Filton-built wings for the Airbus A320 nearing completion in the East Bay of the assembly hall.*

Opposite: *A United Airways 150-seat Airbus A320, flies high on wings designed and built at Filton.*

Gloucestershire Aircraft Company

It was a tall, bearded hook-nosed young man named George Holt-Thomas who began it all. The son of the owner of the *Daily Graphic*, he soon realised in 1910 that the new sport of flying would be a valuable source of news stories for the paper. To find out more about aeroplanes and flying he talked to other young men in the business. Tom Sopwith, Robert Blackburn, Freddy Handley Page and the dour Short brothers. He also visited France and met Henri and Maurice Farman, two Englishmen who lived and built aeroplanes there. These all fired Holt-Thomas's enthusiasm for aviation. In 1911 the Farmans gave him a licence to sell their aeroplanes in the UK. His success in this role earned him a licence from the Seguin brothers in France to handle sales of their Gnome rotary engines. The following year he formed the Aircraft Manufacturing Co. at Hendon with an engine factory at Walthamstow and a third at Merton where a subsidiary company, Airships Ltd, could produce balloons and airships.

Aware of his own lack of engineering and management skills Holt-Thomas sought men who had them. At the Balloon Factory at Farnborough was young Hugh Burroughes who

The woodshop in H.H. Martyn's factory at Sunningend, Cheltenham during 1914. It was here that, later, all wood was prepared for the company's aircraft department.

had translated the Farman and Gnome technical manuals into English and was highly regarded there. In March 1914 Burroughes became general manager of the Aircraft Manufacturing Co. (Airco). Another recruit was the modest but gifted young Geoffrey de Havilland who joined in June. Then, at midnight on 4 August Great Britain declared war on Germany. Airco still needed a designer. De Havilland (DH) had been called up, but he was perceived to be of much more value to the nation working with Airco than as a squadron pilot and he returned to the company.

It was not until an order for 250 DH.2 single-seat scout aircraft was received that Burroughes and Holt-Thomas realised that Airco's manufacturing facilities couldn't cope with the rate of deliveries demanded. As aircraft structures were mainly of wood the place to look for additional facilities was a reputable woodworking company. Burroughes asked the firm which supplied Airco's wood where to look and was directed to H.H. Martyn & Co. Ltd. He visited Martyn's Sunningend factory on the outskirts of Cheltenham in April 1915, liked the serious A.W. Martyn, its managing director, and was impressed by the skill of the craftsmen and their equipment. A few weeks later Airco placed a trial order for Maurice Farman Longhorn and Shorthorn aircraft spares and components with H.H. Martyn. This resulted in large contracts for DH.2s and for BE.2c and DH.4 bombers and DH.6 trainers. In early 1917 Burroughes and A.W. Martyn formed a new joint company to build aeroplanes. In this way the Gloucestershire Aircraft Co. Ltd (GAC) began life on 5 June 1917 with £10,000 capital. Some 800 DH.9 bombers, Bristol F.2b Fighters, FE.2bs and Nieuport Nighthawks were built, some of this work being sub-contracted to Daniels & Co. in Stroud and Gloucester Carriage & Wagon Co. in the city. Test flying was done at an Air Board Aircraft Acceptance Park at Brockworth.

At the war's end in November 1918 military contracts dried up, but GAC bought a large number of Nieuport Nighthawk components, showing its determination to stay in the aircraft business. When the British Nieuport company closed in November 1920 its chief designer, Harry P. Folland, joined GAC. 'HP' had worked at Farnborough (the Balloon Factory having become the Royal Aircraft Factory) where he had designed the SE.4, SE.5 and then the SE.5a regarded by many as the finest single-seat fighter of the war. Under his guidance, using the stored Nighthawk components, sixty Sparrowhawk fighters and trainers were produced for the Imperial Japanese Navy. There they took-off from wooden platforms on top of warships' gun turrets. This export order confirmed GAC as a 'player' in the aviation business, but did little to promote the company in the eyes of the Air Board as a builder of high-performance aircraft. So Folland turned to racing aircraft.

The result was the Mars I, a sleek little biplane using Nighthawk components. At some stage it was dubbed the 'Bamel'. The story has it that when Folland took Burroughes to see it being built, the rear fuselage lacked its fabric covering and was bare. Burroughes commented that the large structure housing the fuel tank was like a camel's hump. By combining the words 'bare' or 'bear' with 'camel' the result was 'bamel'. This mythical beast was depicted on the fuselage, having a bear's hindquarters with fin and rudder plus the hump and fore-end of a camel. Astride it was J.H. 'Jimmy' James, the GAC pilot, with his customary white scarf trailing. Conceived and built in only four weeks it won the June 1921 Aerial Derby at 163.3mph, set a British speed record at 196.4mph in December and won the following year's Aerial Derby at 177.85mph. It achieved 212mph in an attempt on

H.P. Folland, Gloster's chief engineer and designer 1921-37, was rarely separated from his pipe, even in the company of his wife.

With its Napier Lion engine at 'full chat' the Mars I is seen at Villesauvage in September 1922 for the Coupe Deutsch race. J.H. James, the pilot, lost his way when his maps blew away. Note the aircraft's very 'clean' lines.

James in the cockpit of the Mars I. The 'half-bear, half-camel' motif on the fuselage side reflects the Mars' nickname 'Bamel'.

Nighthawks being converted to Mars X standard in the Assembly Shop at Sunningend. Nightjars are being assembled in the background.

Only one Grouse was built in 1923. A private venture research aircraft it investigated flight handling characteristics of Folland's combinations of upper- and lower-wing aerofoil sections.

The diminutive Gannet weighed only 283lb. With wings folded for easy housing it is seen when powered by a 7hp two-cylinder Burney & Blackburne Tomtit engine.

A pair of Jaguar-engined Grebe fighters of No.25 Squadron get airborne from RAF Hawkinge, Kent.

the World Speed Record – failing by only 2.4mph to beat the existing one. Renamed Gloster I it won the 1923 Aerial Derby at 192.4mph. Mounted on floats, RAF pilots flew it while practising for the 1925 and 1927 Schneider Trophy Contests. When James left GAC he became a technical representative with S. Smith & Sons, instrument makers. But, as noted on an earlier page, more of Mr Smith later.

Folland's development of new aerofoil wing sections bore fruit when a Sparrowhawk airframe, renamed the Grouse, test flew them in 1923. Three prototypes were ordered by the Air Ministry and became the forerunners of a series of fighter biplanes. But, first, there was the Gannet, a diminutive biplane built for the October 1923 *Daily Mail* Light Aeroplane Trials. Weighing only 283lb it had a 750cc two-cylinder two-stroke air-cooled engine designed by Sir John Carden, a young amateur engineer. The Gannet was broken up by a scrap merchant in 1929.

The first of the three prototypes mentioned above had a 350hp Armstrong Siddeley Motors Jaguar engine and became the Grebe single-seat fighter prototype of which 126 were built during 1922-25. Grebes were the first Gloster aircraft to be built in quantity for the RAF. They equipped five squadrons and were used for air-launching trials from airships. On 21 October 1926 two Grebes were carried aloft under the airship R–33, were released and then flown back to two air stations. Three Grebes were sold to New Zealand. The type was withdrawn from RAF service in July 1929.

With the end of the Aerial Derbies GAC sought other sales promotional events. In the summer of 1924 two Gloster II racing floatplanes were built for the Schneider Trophy Contest in Baltimore, USA which was cancelled when only the US team was entered.

The H.H. Martyn/ Gloucestershire Aircraft Co.'s factory at Sunningend, Cheltenham. The large 'signpost' on the roof points to the Hucclecote aerodrome and factory in 1927.

The Gloster IIA floatplane at the Marine Aircraft Experimental Establishment, Felixstowe, Suffolk. Built for the 1925 Schneider Trophy Contest at Baltimore, Hubert Broad flew it into second place.

Eleven Gamecock Is of No.23 Squadron and their air and ground crews at RAF Kenley, Surrey in 1927. Douglas Bader joined this squadron in August 1930.

A Gamecock II, flown by Howard Saint, Gloster's test pilot, takes off from Hucclecote in 1927.

Using the Grebe as a starting point Folland then designed a larger more powerful single-seat fighter. This emerged as the Gamecock, the first one being flown by Howard Saint, GAC's pilot, early in February 1925. A total of ninety-five Gamecocks were built for the RAF. In late 1927 the Finnish Government bought two 'pattern' Gamecocks and a licence to build the type in Helsinki's National Aircraft Factory. Renamed the 'Kukko', fifteen were built beginning in 1928. The last one was withdrawn from service in September 1944.

By 1926 Gloucestershire Aircraft Co. had become well known in the British aircraft industry and overseas – where its name caused problems. As Burroughes said, 'Once you leave Dover nobody can pronounce it'. So he changed it. On 11 November it became the Gloster Aircraft Co. But this wasn't the only change. GAC's board realised that the physical and technical requirements for all-metal aircraft construction and those of H.H. Martyn's woodworking and architectural work were incompatible; moreover, GAC was using a hangar at the Aircraft Acceptance Park and, in effect, was running two factories some seven miles apart. Thus, it was decided to move all aircraft work from Sunningend to Brockworth. This took about five years to complete, but was not universally popular. Headlines in Cheltenham's *Gloucestershire Echo* screamed 'one can't take a wages bill of £2,500 per week out of the Town without it making a difference'. The *Gloucester Citizen* rejoiced 'One of the biggest and most important air industries in the British Isles will shortly be established in its entirety at works within ten minutes drive of Gloucester ... it is anticipated that a greater part of the weekly wages will be spent in the City and its vicinity'.

An interesting little sidelight on this move involved a decision about GAC's new postal address. The site straddled the boundary line between the parishes of Brockworth and Hucclecote. However, there were two daily postal deliveries to Hucclecote, and only one in Brockworth, so Hucclecote became GAC's new home!

During the lengthy move two Gloster III racing floatplanes were built for the 1925 Schneider Trophy Contest in Baltimore again. Both went to the USA but one was damaged during test flying. The other one, flown by Hubert Broad, came second at 199.167mph, behind the US Curtiss R34C-2, which was 33mph faster. Three experimental single-seat fighters named Gorcocks, were next in line. They flight-tested metal and wood structures, Napier Lion engines and various radiators. Three more, named the Guan, were built especially to test supercharging systems on the Lion. These all flew between mid-summer 1925–27.

These prototypes provided work for only a small number of employees; but help was at hand. The de Havilland Co. had no success with several military prototypes and had problems with a civil air survey aircraft, the DH.67. This was transferred to GAC at

J7503, with an all-metal airframe was one of three Gorcock experimental fighters used to test different Napier Lion engines and wood or metal structures. All had two fuselage-mounted guns.

Hucclecote where, redesignated the Gloster AS.31, two examples were built. The first one was accidentally first flown in June 1929. During what were to have been taxiing trials, Saint opened the throttles a bit too much and found himself airborne and heading for a hangar! Nevertheless, he managed a careful circuit and landing. This AS.31 surveyed 63,000 square miles of what was then Northern Rhodesia starting in 1931; the second one was flown at Farnborough, now renamed the Royal Aircraft Establishment, on lengthy trials of wireless telegraphy systems and equipment.

Meanwhile, the Air Ministry had given GAC responsibility for development of all de Havilland's military designs. Thus, in early 1931 Gloster was working on the 95ft span DH.72 three-engined heavy bomber. It was completed and first flown on 28 July 1931. From September 1930 the DH.77 single-seat monoplane fighter designed by George Carter, was based at Hucclecote for a 100-hour flight development programme on its 300hp Napier Rapier engine. It was withdrawn from use late in 1934.

With few contracts for new military aircraft being awarded, seven companies submitted designs to meet a requirement for a general purpose aeroplane. The specification wanted maximum use of components from the type it was to replace – the ageing DH.9A. Gloster's Goral used its wings and several other pieces but it didn't win the contract. This went to Westland Aircraft's Wapiti. However, through Gloster's subsidiary The Steel Wing Co., the Hucclecote factory got orders worth £330,000 from Westland for 525 sets of all-metal structured Wapiti wings. While working on the Goral, GAC produced the Goring two-seat day bomber able to have wheeled landing gear or floats. Again, it was built only as a prototype.

The second Gloster AS.31 aerial survey aircraft. The first one operated in this role; this one undertook wireless telegraphy proving flights at Farnborough.

On wheels the Goring was an ugly duckling, but on floats it was almost a swan. Here it taxies on choppy water, possibly at Felixstowe.

Between 1925 and 1936 GAC developed and produced several types of hydraulically-operated variable-pitch propellers designed by Dr Hele-Shaw and Mr T.E. Beacham but failed to win orders from any engine or aircraft manufacturer. Then in 1929 the Air Ministry ordered twelve propellers for testing and a Gamecock with a Bristol Jupiter engine flew a seventy-five-hour programme. In the same year, wealthy Italian residents in England financed Gloster's construction of a unique aircraft wing designed by Ugo Antoni, an Italian engineer. It was built in three separate sections to be flexible so that its aerofoil section could be changed in flight by the pilot. It was fitted to an Italian-built Breda 15 high-wing monoplane and was first flown by Rex Stocken on 8 September 1933. Sadly, Saint flew it on 1 December without consulting Stocken and crashed it in severe turbulence around nearby Chosen Hill. Early in 1929 a young Swiss engineer, H.J. Steiger, gave an order to GAC for the construction of a monospar-structured wing. To prove it, he designed a small twin-engined cabin monoplane which was named the Gloster Monospar SS.1 which flew in October 1930. The Air Ministry then ordered a 63ft-span monospar wing for the RAF's three-engined Fokker VIIA/3m transport which was fitted in September 1931 and first flew on 16 December at Hucclecote.

While these disparate prototypes were being built GAC designed and built the Goldfinch which was an all-metal Gamecock. Then Folland used wooden construction for the Gloster IV floatplane for the 1927 Schneider Trophy Contest in Venice. An aerodynamically-clean biplane, Folland had reduced the Gloster III's head resistance by forty per cent and increased the top speed by 70mph. Three Gloster IVs were ordered each costing £8,250. In the contest on 26 September the Gloster IV, flown by Flt Lt Sam Kinkhead of the RAF High Speed Flight, suffered a cracked propeller shaft on the sixth lap. He had, however, set a record for biplanes in the contest series with a 277mph third lap.

While the Gloster IV was being designed a Japanese company, Nakajima Hikoki K.K. enquired about licenced production of the Gamecock to replace the Navy's Sparrowhawks. This was a non-starter, but Folland was offering a private-venture naval fighter to the Air Ministry. When it failed to win an order he offered it to the Japanese. Again, he reverted to wooden structures for the Gambet which closely followed the Gamecock's design. In a fly-off between the Gambet and other Japanese aeroplanes Folland's aircraft won hands-down. A total of 150 A1N1s and A1N2s, as they were redesignated, were built by Nakajima in Japan.

The Gnatsnapper single-seat deck-landing fighter of 1929 was the victim of countless modifications, changes and failures of engines and pilot 'finger trouble' during evaluation in 1929-31. Meanwhile the Gloster VI monoplane floatplane for the 1929 Schneider

In 1929 Gloster Aircraft built special 'bird wings' designed by Ugo Antoni, an Italian aircraft engineer. They were fitted to this Breda 15, but it was 8 September 1933 before it flew.

Although a biplane, Folland's Napier Lion-engined Gloster IVA for the 1927 Schneider Trophy Contest in Venice was a very clean design.

Contest on the Solent was being built. This time Folland used an all-metal fuselage with wooden wings. Again, his aeroplane was beautifully streamlined and looked a winner but...! This time the Napier Lion engine could not be cajoled to keep running smoothly when going round corners, despite the ministrations of Napier, Gloster and RAF engineers; so the aeroplane was withdrawn from the contest. Using the Lion's ability to deliver power when flying straight and level, the Gloster VI set a world speed record averaging 336.3mph when flown by Flt Lt George H. Stainforth on 10 September.

Until the mid-1920s the design and performance of the RAF's front-line single-seat fighters had advanced very little when compared with those used in the First World War. When the Fairey Fox two-seat light bomber with its US-built Curtiss D-12 engine entered RAF service it was faster than the latest fighters! This alerted the Air Ministry to the pressing need of replacements for those already in service. In April 1926 Specification F.9/26 was issued calling for a new all-metal day and night fighter. Gloster proposed the Goldfinch but the Bristol Bulldog won the contract, thus perpetuating the old two-gun biplane concept.

Meanwhile, Folland was designing a new fighter, the SS18, which was a Bristol Mercury radial-engined two-bay biplane. Howard Saint first got it airborne in January 1929. There followed many months of flight testing with various engines and airframe modifications during which this prototype was designated the SS18A, SS18B, SS19, SS19A and SS19B. Its original two-gun armament was increased to four guns, then to six when it was dubbed

Several different engines were flown in the two Gnatsnapper deck-landing fighter prototypes; this one has a Rolls-Royce Goshawk evaporatively-cooled engine.

While being launched at Calshot in August 1929, the first Gloster VI gives way to another 'racer', the Mauretania, *moving up Southampton Water.*

the 'multi-gun fighter'. Then the Air Ministry wanted four of them removed! It was September 1933 before twenty-four of these aircraft were ordered for the RAF with the name Gauntlet. Eventually 228 were produced.

By the mid-1930s Gloster's financial resources had been drained away by the production of a series of prototypes which had failed to win orders. In an attempt to earn money, large areas of the factory were converted to badminton courts alongside mushroom beds and pig-sties. Elsewhere, motor car bodies, milk churns, fish-frying equipment and tracked motorised barrows were being built. The long list of prototypes included the big TC.33 troop carrier/bomber and the TSR.38 torpedo bomber. Then Hawker Aircraft, whose Kingston-on-Thames factory was overflowing with work, took over Gloster Aircraft Co., thus laying the foundation of what was to become the Hawker Siddeley Group. By the end of 1934 production of Hawker aeroplanes designed by Sydney Camm was well established. A total of 146 Harts, Hardys, Audax and Hartbees were built at Hucclecote, where there were factory expansions, with Gauntlet production alongside them. The Danish Government licence-built seventeen Gauntlets during 1936-38. Eighteen RAF squadrons and five Auxiliary Air Force squadrons flew Gauntlets which were their last open-cockpit fighters. Almost certainly the last recorded RAF use of Gauntlets came as late as May 1943 when four were taken on charge as trainers by a Meteorological Flight at Eastleigh, Nairobi and flew from there for some months thereafter.

The SS19A was the penultimate development configuration before this aeroplane, J9125, became the Gauntlet prototype in July 1933.

Five Gauntlet IIs of No.56 Squadron fly in a line-abreast formation.

J9125 on test in the Royal Aircraft Establishment's 24ft wind tunnel at Farnborough.

Jack Johnstone, experimental department foreman, gives scale to the Gloster TC.33 troop-carrier/bomber in 1932. Note the push-me-pull-you Goshawk engine installation and enclosed flight deck.

The Gloster SS37 was largely built using Gauntlet components. Here it has the original engine cowling and discs on the Dowty internally-sprung wheels.

Above: *Gladiator L8032 with a new serial after restoration to airworthy condition during 1959-60. Here it flies to the Shuttleworth Trust on 7 November 1960 piloted by Wing Commander R.F. 'Dickie' Martin, chief test pilot.*

Opposite
Above: *One of the second batch of Gladiator 1s outside the Flight Shed at Hucclecote in 1937. The presence of ladies in hats and of children suggests that it is a special day at the factory.*

Below: Faith, *the restored fuselage of one of the legendary three Malta Gladiators, conveys Grp Capt M.J. Armitage, Station Commander, as he leaves RAF Luqa. This Gladiator was presented to the Malta National War Museum.*

Known unofficially as the 'Unnamed Fighter' the Gloster F.5/34 monoplane fighter was Folland's last design for the company. It owed some of its features to the Gladiator, particularly the Bristol Mercury engine, cockpit canopy and tailplane.

The issue of Specification F.7/30 called for an all-metal single-engined single-seat day and night fighter having a 250mph top speed at 15,000ft, a 50mph landing speed, and armed with four .303in machine guns. It was clear that the winning design would be ordered in very large numbers. Seven companies submitted about a dozen designs. Gloster was not among them as Folland was too busy with Gauntlet development to do more than keep a careful eye on what the others were doing. By 1933 he had a mental picture of a likely F.7/30 contender. Using a Gauntlet as the notional starting point he replaced its two-bay wings with single-bays, and the multi-strut landing gear with two cantilever legs and Dowty internally-sprung wheels, and added two under-wing guns to the pair in the fuselage. Roy Fedden at Bristol had promised early delivery of a new 700hp Mercury radial engine. With this power and the cleaned-up airframe, Folland was confident of achieving the 250mph top speed. Meanwhile, other manufacturers were having serious problems with engine failures, cracked fuselages and crashes. The Air Ministry's long-running attempt to get a high-performance fighter had collapsed. As the new monoplane fighters could not be

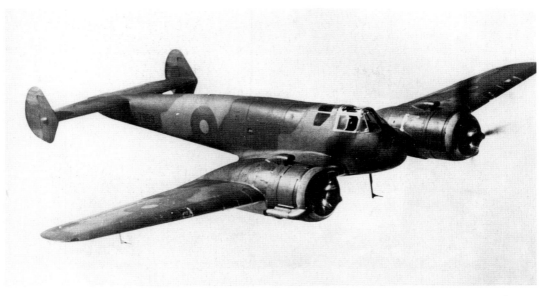

The Gloster F.9/37 single-seat fighter, with Bristol Taurus engines, Dowty landing gear, Rotol propellers and Smiths instrumentation, was first flown by Gerry Sayer on 3 April 1939.

ready until 1937, Gloster quickly modified a Gauntlet to embody Folland's envisaged features, and on 12 September 1934 Gerry Sayer, Gloster's test pilot, flew it for the first time. When the RAF evaluated it the top speed requirement was not met, but when a more powerful Mercury engine was installed the 250mph was attainable. As a stop-gap fighter the Gladiator, as it was named, did a good job. More than 450 were built for the RAF and 98 for the Royal Navy. It operated in the UK, Middle East and North Africa and off Royal Navy carriers. It was exported to nine overseas countries who bought 165 new aircraft. The Gladiator was the RAF's last biplane fighter.

Folland's first monoplane fighter was designed to meet Specification F.5/34 which led to the development of the Hurricane and the Spitfire. Dubbed the Gloster 'Unnamed Fighter', it was virtually an all-metal monoplane Gladiator. Folland jettisoned the top wing, used a thicker bottom wing to house the retractable landing gear and eight machine guns while the Mercury radial engine, sliding cockpit canopy and tail unit were almost Gladiator look-alikes.

Building the prototype took a long time. Then, in January 1937, Folland left Gloster and joined British Marine Aircraft Ltd at Hamble. He was succeeded by George Carter from de Havilland who took over responsibility for completing the new fighter's construction. Gerry Sayer flew the F.5/34 in late December 1937, only a few days before the RAF received its first Hawker Hurricanes. Needless to say, the F.5/34 prototype was abandoned.

George Carter's first Gloster design was the F.9/37 twin-engined monoplane fighter with Bristol Taurus radial engines which first flew on 3 April 1938. The specification was for a heavy forward-firing armament and Carter met this with two 20mm cannon in the nose

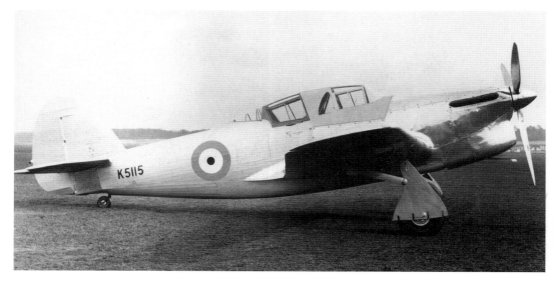

The first Hawker Henley prototype at Brooklands in 1937. During 1938-39 Gloster Aircraft built all of the 200 production Henleys ordered for the RAF.

Hawker Hurricanes being built in Gloster's Hucclecote factory in 1941. Production totalled 2,750 Hurricanes plus many repaired aircraft.

This Hawker Typhoon 1B was just one of the 3,330 Typhoons built by Gloster Aircraft, which was the sole production source for these fighter/bombers, during 1942-45.

and three more firing over the pilot's cockpit canopy. This made it the most heavily-armed fighter in the world at that time. The second prototype had Rolls-Royce Peregrine inline engines. Though both performed well, neither was ordered.

In October 1938 production of 200 Hawker Henley two-seat aircraft began at Hucclecote. All the preparatory work for assembly of 600 Armstrong Whitworth Albemarle twin-engined aircraft also was done by Gloster before handover to the newly formed A.W. Hawkesley company using the Brockworth shadow factory, about 300yds across the airfield.

Before production of the Henleys ended, work on the Hurricane began. Seven weeks after the Second World War broke out on 3 September 1939 the first Gloster-built Hurricane was rolled off the line. By the end of October 1940 the 1,000th aircraft had been built with peak production rate being achieved that month when 160 new Hurricanes and 8 repaired aircraft were completed. By early 1941 GAC had some 50 acres of floor space and 14,000 employees. The last of 2,750 Hurricanes built at Hucclecote flew in March 1942. Ten months' production of the Hawker Typhoon at Hucclecote became the sole source of production Typhoons. The first was flown by Michael Daunt, a Gloster pilot, on 27 May 1941. Production peaked with 1,165 Typhoons built during 1944 and ended in November 1945 when 3,330 Typhoons had been built by GAC.

While this gigantic production programme rolled on for some six years, other historic events were taking place. In August 1939 George Carter was asked by the Ministry to design a jet-propelled aircraft. He asked to see the engine running and went to Power Jets' Lutterworth factory near Rugby. Afterwards he said that he had never seen a more unpromising contraption. Years later he told the author 'It got red hot when they ran it at

Britain's and the Allies' first jet aeroplane, the still-unpainted Gloster E.28/39, photographed at the Bentham dispersal factory in 1941. Note the Dowty tricycle landing gear, fabric-covered rudder and nose air intake for the Whittle jet engine in the fuselage with its heat-sensitive strips.

Gerry Sayer takes the E.28/39 into the air at RAF Cranwell for its first flight on 15 May 1941. This long-distance photograph, taken by Gloster test pilot Neil 'Michael' Daunt, is the only one showing this historic event.

It is believed that this photograph of the E.28/39, a colour print, was taken at Bentham before this little aeroplane was presented to London's Science Museum on 28 April 1946.

full speed and I expected it to catch fire'. On a subsequent visit he got a much more favourable impression of Frank Whittle's amazing engine.

On 3 February 1940 GAC received a contract to build two prototype jet aircraft to Specification E.28/39. They materialised as small, low-winged monoplanes with the engine buried amidships in the fuselage aft of the cockpit, a nose air intake and a tricycle landing gear. The primary object of the E.28/39 was to 'flight test the engine installation', however the contract also added 'but the design will be based on the requirements for a fixed-gun interceptor fighter as far as limitations on size and weight imposed by the power unit permit'. One wonders what compelling reason would have caused the Air Ministry to order Gloster to fit four guns and 2,000 rounds of ammunition in this little prototype, knowing its very limited internal space and the amount of power its engine was then producing.

This aeroplane first got daylight under its Dowty wheels on 8 April 1941 at Hucclecote when Gerry Sayer made three 'straights'. On each one it lifted 6ft off the grass airfield for 100-200yd 'hops'. The first flight took place at RAF Cranwell, Lincolnshire on 15 May where Sayer made a highly successful seventeen-minute test flight. This must surely rank alongside the Wright Brothers' first sustained, powered and controlled flight at Kittyhawk on 17 December 1903.

Some months before metal was cut for the E.28/39, George Carter was producing designs for an operational jet fighter. Without having seen a jet aircraft fly he was aware

This Meteor 1, EE223/G, was the first to fly with Derwent I engines in short nacelles. The sideways-opening cockpit canopy and high tailplane are noteworthy features.

The world's first propeller-turbine aircraft was this Meteor I with Rolls-Royce Trent engines driving Rotol propellers. It was first flown by Eric Greenwood, Gloster's chief test pilot on 20 September 1945.

A line-up of Meteor I and III fighters of No.616 Squadron at Lubeck, Germany in May 1945. The nearest aircraft is having its main 325-gallon fuel tank refilled from the bowser.

Gloster's private venture Meteor 7 carmine two-seat trainer demonstrator first flew on 19 March 1948 and toured European and Middle-East countries.

A Meteor 3 with Rolls-Royce Derwent V engines, lands on HMS Implacable *during deck-landing trials in March 1948. The Meteor was the first twin-jet aircraft to land on a Royal Navy aircraft carrier.*

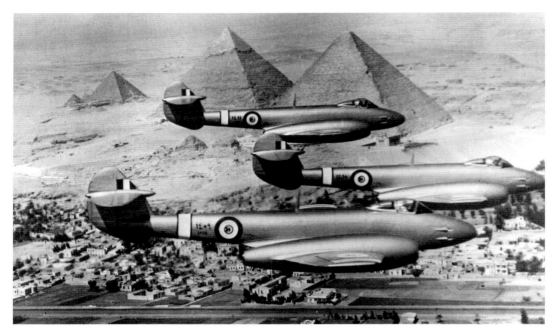

A neat 'vic' of Egyptian Air Force Meteor 4s fly past the Pyramids in 1950.

Production of Meteor T.7 trainers and F.8 fighters in Hucclecote's erecting shop in January 1951. Front fuselages are on a tracked assembly line with centre-sections on the right.

Based on the Meteor 8 the Ground Attack Fighter, dubbed 'The Reaper', carries twenty-four rocket projectiles and wing-tip fuel tanks. It could also carry four 1,000lb bombs.

Meteor 8s of No.500 (County of Kent) Squadron, Royal Auxiliary Air Force, 'break' before landing at RAF West Malling in 1953.

Pilotless Meteor 4s, converted to U15 target aircraft, flew during guided-missile development programmes. The wing-tip pods carry cameras. The first pilotless take-off was on 17 January 1955.

that, because jet-engine power was comparatively puny, the fighter would need two engines to provide the required performance. In November 1940 the Air Ministry issued Specification F.9/40 for a six-cannon jet fighter with provision for a pressure suit for the pilot. Carter persuaded the Air Staff to accept four-cannon armament and promised to investigate the pressure suit installation at a later date.

Following the submission of George Carter's preliminary brochure, the Ministry of Aircraft Production (MAP) order for twelve 'Gloster Whittle aeroplanes' to Specification F.9/40 was received on 7 February 1941. The contract also required the manufacture of jigs and tools to enable eighty aircraft per month to be built. Following many problems with the engine production programme the first flight of a Gloster F.9/40 took place at RAF Cranwell on 5 March 1943 with Michael Daunt as pilot. Then there was the year-long haggle before the name Meteor was agreed for this new aeroplane. By then 300 aircraft had been ordered and production was in progress. Thus began a twelve-year programme during which 3,545 Meteors were built in the UK and Holland. There were fourteen different Meteor variants, being built as day and night fighters, fighter reconnaissance and unarmed reconnaissance aircraft, as trainers, target-towers and unmanned target aircraft. No less than twenty-one different power units, from turbojets and turboprops to ramjets and rocket motors, were fitted to Meteors. They flew with thirty-two RAF squadrons and countless other units and with the Fleet Air Arm. Meteors were exported to twelve other countries. Two world speed records, two closed-circuit records, five capital-to-capital records and time-to-height records

The first prototype GA.5, WD804, the forerunner of the Javelin, seen at Gloster's Moreton Valence factory and airfield in September 1951. Note the nose pitot boom and anti-spin parachute-housing on top of the tailplane.

This view of the first prototype Gloster E.1/44 fighter reveals the clean lines of its corpulent fuselage and comparatively small air intakes for its 5,000lb thrust Rolls-Royce Nene engine.

WT830, the fourth prototype GA.5 reveals its modified wing planform with a kinked leading edge.

were all set by Meteors. They fought in the Second World War and in Korea; they were flown by the Argentine Air Force in a local fracas and it is alleged that Egyptian Air Force Meteors operated in the Suez Campaign. The last Gloster-built Meteor left Hucclecote on 9 April 1954 flown by Jim Cooksey, the company's chief production test pilot.

With this great record of success it interesting to note that, in 1942, the MAP had considered cancelling the Gloster F.9/40 prototypes in favour of a single-engined project to meet Specification E.5/42. In November 1943 Gloster began work on two GA.1 airframes but this was abandoned when Specification E.1/44 was issued the following year. Three Gloster E.1/44s were built; the first one *did* 'fall off the back of a lorry' and was scrapped, the others were test flown but their performance was not good, their development potential was poor and they were eventually scrapped too.

Gloster's last aeroplane was the Javelin, built to meet Specification F.4/48 for a high-performance two-seat all-weather fighter equipped with radar, four 30mm cannon and air-to-air guided missiles. In April 1949 the Ministry of Supply instructed Gloster to proceed with the manufacture of four prototypes. As an economy measure this order was reduced to two aircraft. The sheer impossibility of completing the flight development of such a complex aeroplane with two prototypes was eventually realised. Fortunately this instruction was

XA568 and XA570, two of the first three Javelin 1 all-weather fighters delivered to the RAF, leave Moreton Valence on 31 December 1955.

The 500-yard long erecting shop at Hucclecote with Javelin airframes being assembled on the tracked production lines. Some 7,000 aircraft were built here between 1939 and 1959.

A Javelin prepared for engine-running in the Hucclecote silencing pen before the main doors were closed. A similar pen was built at Moreton Valence.

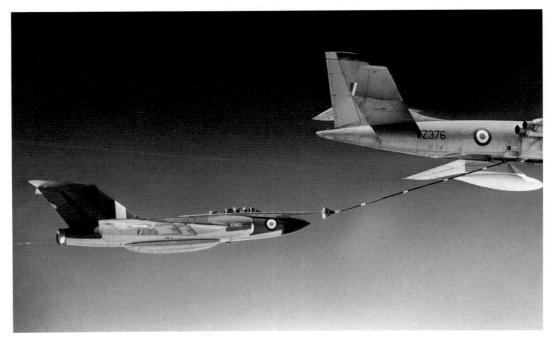

XH965, the last production Javelin 9 with a 20ft-long refuelling probe, was used for in-flight refuelling trials with a Valiant tanker aircraft. Note the two 250-gallon 'bosom' tanks under the fuselage.

changed to six aircraft, but the entire development programme was seriously delayed. The first prototype, now named Javelin, was completed in July 1951 and was first flown on 26 November at Gloster's Moreton Valence airfield by Bill Waterton, chief test pilot. When Dick Walker, who had been responsible for this aeroplane's design, asked Waterton how it had handled he replied 'Well, she went up and she came down'. The rest he put in his flight report!

The Javelin was of unorthodox appearance having a large delta wing, a tall swept broad-chord fin with a delta tailplane on top. The two Armstrong Siddeley Sapphire engines were mounted in the deep fuselage with air intakes mounted on its flanks ahead of the wing leading edge. This prototype began the lengthy test programme until, during the 99th flight on 29 June 1952 when, being flown at high speed, both elevators were lost following violent flutter. Bravely, Waterton stayed with his aircraft, used the variable incidence tailplane to provide some control and managed a very high-speed landing on the long main runway at Boscombe Down, during which the landing gear collapsed. He was awarded the George Medal for 'courage beyond the call of duty' and saving the auto-observer records.

First deliveries of the Javelin Mk 1 to the RAF began in February 1956 when No.46 Squadron at RAF Odiham began a 1,000-hour intensive flying programme. A total of 430 production Javelins were built in nine variants. They flew with eighteen RAF squadrons and numerous training and development establishments, operating in Europe, the Mediterranean region, the Middle and Far East and Central Africa. No.60 Squadron based at RAF Tengah, Singapore was the last operational unit to fly Javelins. This squadron marked its disbandment on 30 April 1968 with a unique fly-past in the dark with reheats blazing.

But some four years before that dramatic fly-past of Gloster's last aircraft, the company had predeceased the Javelin. Back in 1952 Dick Walker was already working on a new all-weather fighter for the RAF. This was the Javelin thin-wing development (TWD) over which much 'midnight oil' was burned and many differing designs proposed. Ultimately, in May 1956 Gloster submitted designs for a true supersonic fighter capable of Mach 1.3. It was powered with two Olympus B.Ol.21R engines each with 29,000lb thrust, had 60ft 8in-span wings and a 50,500lb operational weight. Metal had already been cut on the first of eighteen development TWD Javelins when in July 1956 Gloster received notification of its cancellation.

During its final years Gloster turned to a variety of non-aviation products including vending machines, light alloy lamp-posts, small fire-fighting vehicles, commercial vehicle bodies and agricultural forage harvesters. Dicky Martin, Gloster's chief test pilot, flew the Aviation Traders' Accountant twin turboprop short-haul passenger prototype with the possibility that Gloster might produce it. He was not enthusiastic about its handling and performance and Gloster was instructed to hand over the aeroplane and all flight reports to A.V. Roe at Manchester. On 8 April 1960 the last Javelin and Gloster's last aeroplane was flown away from Hucclecote. Then on 6 April 1964 the Hucclecote factory was sold to become an industrial trading estate and Gloster Aircraft Co. slipped quietly into the history books.

N7511, one of a batch of 150 Parnall Panther two-seat deck-landing reconnaissance/spotter aircraft built by British & Colonial Aeroplane Co. at Filton during 1919-20.

The civilianised variant of the Plover carrier-born fighter, G-EBON, outside the flight shed at Yate. It was a competitor in the 1926 King's Cup Race but failed to complete the course.

The lone Pike naval reconnaissance prototype being prepared for flight testing in June 1927. Note the heavy Warren girder-style wing bracing and dihedral root of top wing.

Designed to be carried in a submarine, the 1925 Peto's wings could be folded for a snug fit in the vessel's hangar. (Ken Wixey)

Numbered 14 for the September 1923 Light Aeroplane Trials, the Pixie III two-seater, G-EBJG, on the Yate airfield. Below, its neat engine installation can be seen.

Sharply angled single interplane struts and swept top wing are notable features of the 1928 Imp sport aircraft. (Ken Wixey)

Parnall & Sons Ltd

Like many small family businesses established during the nineteenth century, with the passage of time the fortunes, activities and locations of the Parnall & Sons company were subject to many changes.

This Bristol company was established by William Parnall in 1820 in the weights and measures business. Some years later it diversified into shop fronts and later still became Parnall & Sons Ltd. In 1898 it was bought by W&T Avery, a well-known scales and weighing machine manufacturer. The Parnall family was still a force to be reckoned with, top management posts being passed on from father to son. When the First World War began in August 1914 George Parnall was managing director of the company which had acquired a sound reputation for the skill of its craftsmen. Inevitably, it was among many which were called upon to build aeroplanes. Inevitably too, new 'factories' were needed, several being set up in various parts of Bristol.

In 1915 Parnall began building a small batch of Short 827 floatplanes. They were followed by some Short Bombers and about fifty-five Hamble Baby floatplanes and landplanes. Parnall's largest wartime sub-contract work was the manufacture of more than 500 Avro 504 bomber and trainer variants. Of more importance, perhaps, was the design and manufacture of two wholly-Parnall types. These were the quaintly named Scout/Zepp Chaser (which never scouted or chased Zeppelins) and the Panther naval reconnaissance biplane. This latter aircraft was designed by Harald Bolas, an accomplished aircraft design

The aggressive-looking Parnall G.4/31 general purpose aircraft at Yate in 1935. (Ken Wixey)

The sixth and last Parnall Heck 2C cabin monoplane, K8853, was supplied to the Air Ministry in 1937, air-tested machine gun installations and became a ground instruction airframe in 1942.

engineer who, in 1917, had joined the company. A small number of Panther prototypes and production aircraft were built by Parnall but the British & Colonial Aeroplane Co. at Filton built some 150 Panthers. Sadly, the production of 'prototypes only' was to be repeated many times in the Parnall story.

After the war George Parnall resigned his post as managing director and set up his own shopfitting business, George Parnall & Co., but he was determined to specialise in aviation work. This required bigger premises and by 1925 this side of his business had moved from Bristol to a small airfield at Yate in Gloucestershire. In 1932 he sold his shopfitting interests to Avery and concentrated wholly on aircraft. Of the twelve designs built during 1921–31 eleven were prototypes only; ten production examples of the other one, the Plover fighter, were built. There was the Puffin and Pipit fighters, the Possum triplane and the Parasol experimental aircraft; for the Navy there were the Perch trainer, Pike reconnaissance aircraft and the Peto floatplane which folded up to fit into a submarine; the little Prawn flying boat's engine could be tilted upwards to clear the spray on take-off. Then there was the burly G.4/31 general purpose biplane. Civil aeroplanes were the diminutive Pixie monoplane, which first flew with a 3hp engine, and the Imp and the Elf two-seater sport biplanes. Tucked in among all these were Cierva Autogiros, de Havilland DH.9As, and a solitary Miles Satyr single-seat aerobatic aircraft. Parnall's biggest production run was the first batch of twenty-three Percival Gull Four three-seat cabin monoplanes.

In 1935 George Parnall sold the company to Nash & Thompson, which produced power-operated gun turrets. There was a change of name, too, Parnall Aircraft Ltd. The family name was too good to lose. And on to the production line came half a dozen Parnall/Hendy Heck three-seat cabin monoplanes, the handsome Parnall Type 382 trainer and the last knockings of the sole G.4/31 which the new owners inherited.

Responding to the RAF expansion programme's needs the Yate factory began building Nash and Thompson gun turrets and five days *before* the Second World War began a Luftwaffe reconaissance aircraft took pictures of the factory for use on another day. Meanwhile, huge numbers of Spitfire wing components, Lancaster rear fuselages and tail units, and Lincoln components were being built with complete sets of Lancaster gun turrets. When three daylight air raids put the Yate factory temporarily out of action and killed many employees, work was dispersed to a number of unlikely places in and around Bristol and into Gloucestershire.

But the Luftwaffe didn't stop Parnall's aircraft component work; it was the outbreak of peace in 1945 which achieved that. Swingeing cuts in contracts, which most of Britain's aircraft industry sustained, were prime reasons for the demise of Parnall Aircraft Ltd. In that year there was a new name over the door. Parnall (Yate) Ltd and domestic equipment and appliances had replaced aeroplane wings and gun turrets.

A.W. Hawkesley Limited

This company was formed in 1940 by the Hawker Siddeley Group to build an aeroplane designed initially by Bristol Aeroplane Co. With the Bristol Type 155 designation it was a mid-wing monoplane bomber with two Bristol Taurus radial engines, twin-fins and rudders, and dorsal and ventral turrets each with two 20mm cannon. Named Albemarle, it was the first British aeroplane to be built in quantity for the RAF with a tricycle landing gear. Bristol designed it to Specification P.9/38 which was replaced by B.17/38. Design responsibility was then transferred to Armstrong Whitworth Aircraft Ltd at Coventry where chief designer John Lloyd made some major changes. Because of the possibilities of a shortage of some specialised metals plus the destruction of aircraft factories by air attack, the AW.41, as this aeroplane was now designated, was redesigned to have wood and steel construction. In addition it was to be built in sections by companies which were not

A night-shift worker busy in 1941 on one of the 600 Albemarles assembled by A.W. Hawkesley in the Brockworth Shadow Factory. (Ray Williams)

V1599, the last of ninety Albemarle GT Mk 1 glider tugs built, became the prototype transport variant. Its Bristol heritage shows in its nose shape and engine installation.

normally in the aircraft-building business. The size of these sections was dictated by the 60ft length of the standard Queen Mary-type articulated road vehicles. Production of the Albemarle was allocated to Gloster's shadow factory at Brockworth.

With initial assistance from Gloster a total of 600 were built in six variants for the RAF. Although they were never flown operationally in their intended role as medium bombers, they operated as glider-tugs or paratroop and cargo transports, taking part in the invasion of Sicily in 1943, the Normandy landings in June 1944 and the Arnhem operation later that year. A number of Albemarles were handed over to the Russian Air Force in 1943.

In addition to these four manufacturer's main factories at Filton, Hucclecote and Yate, in case of an air attack each had large numbers of dispersed 'factories' and design offices scattered throughout Gloucestershire and further afield. These were housed in grand country houses, bus depots, railway arches, a brewery, billiard halls, cider and corset factories, garages, cheese-makers buildings, a soap works and in small purpose-built factories.

Other Aircraft Builders

Although the manufacture of large aeroplanes is no longer carried on in the county, small new aircraft and replicas are still being built by skilled enthusiasts and engineering companies in several locations. The Gloucestershire Aviation Collection has been working for some years on a magnificent Gloster Gamecock replica. This work began in the same buildings in Cheltenham used by Gloucestershire Aircraft Co. some seventy years earlier. In Cam, near Dursley, Retro Track & Air (UK) Ltd has a number of on-going and long-term restoration and construction projects; they include several Gladiators using components rescued from wartime sites in Norway, and a Gamecock. Another project being seriously considered is an airworthy Gloster E.28/39. Retro also is one of the few organisations entrusted with the overhaul of the RAF Battle of Britain Memorial Flight's Rolls-Royce Merlin and Griffon engines for its Hurricane, Spitfires and Lancaster. GAC's Gamecock is nearing completion by the Collection's members in Retro's Cam workshops. A four-year new aircraft-building programme, which began in a garage, was completed at Staverton by a team of four engineers in 2002 when a US kit-plane, a Vans Aircraft RV4, first flew. In addition to these, several other restoration and building projects have been completed at Filton, the Forest of Dean and several other sites in the county, with others under way.

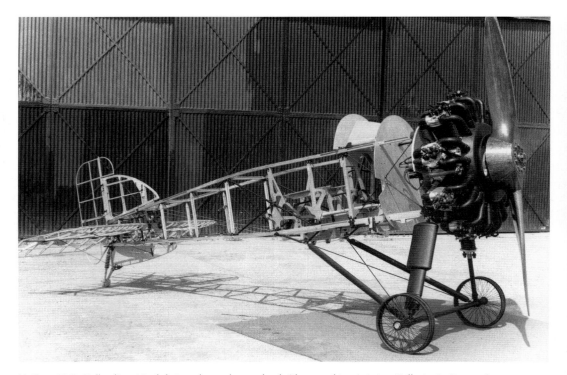

Built to H.P. Folland's original design, the partly completed Gloucestershire Aviation Collection's Gamecock replica as photographed in 1999 with a Bristol Jupiter engine.

Back in 1925 a Cheltenham man's self-built man-powered biplane was a failure but, converted to a monoplane glider, it flew for some 100 yards when ground-launched on Cleeve Hill. In 1951 the author was shown photographs of a biplane glider in the air. Built by two young members of the Royal Observer Corps in the Northleach area, it made several flights over some short distances.

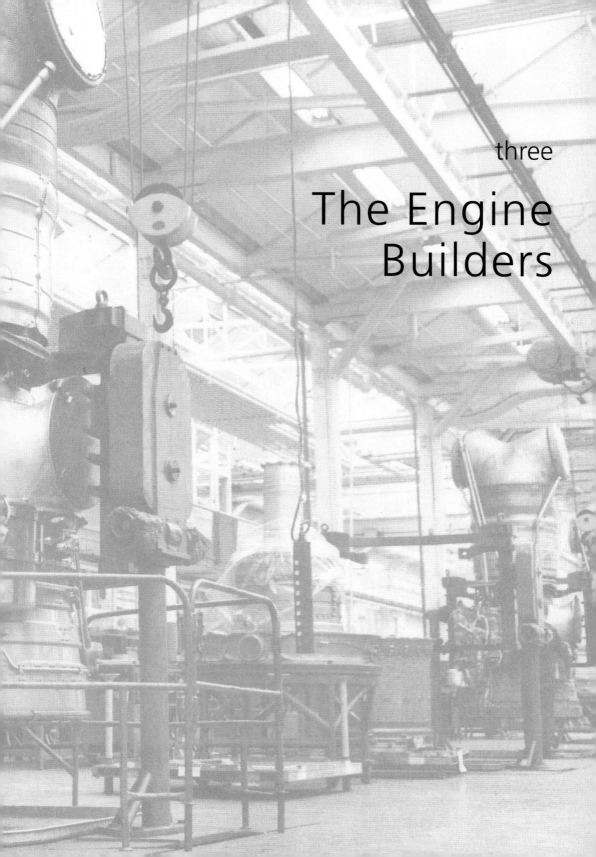

three

The Engine
Builders

Phoenix Radial Rotary Motor Co. Ltd

The roots of this very explicitly named company lay in the Granville Motor Co. in Cheltenham which, in about 1909, moved to premises in Quay Street, Gloucester. While Phoenix produced power units for motor vehicles, it specialised in radial rotary aero-engines in which the cylinders, pistons and crankcase rotated around the stationary crankshaft. This enabled the engine to be cooled while the aircraft was not moving. Engines of this type were being built concurrently by the French Clerget and Gnome companies, by Bentley in England and were being copied in Germany and Japan. Phoenix built 5- or 7-cylinder engines delivering about 50hp and were produced in small quantities against orders. Sadly, when a US business deal went pear-shaped, Phoenix was in financial difficulties and was forced to cease trading in about 1910.

Bristol Aeroplane Company

Having bought the Cosmos Engineering Co. in Fishponds in 1920, Bristol Aeroplane Co. set up its own aero-engine department on 29 July. It was headed by Roy Fedden. But income was less than outgoings and the directors were near a decision to close it having spent £200,000 with little return. Just in time the Jupiter II air-cooled radial engine passed the new severe Air Ministry type test, the first to do so. This saved the engine department's bacon. The Jupiter was a great success, too, at the 1921 Paris Show where the French Gnome-Rhône company bought a licence to build it. Then the RAF ordered eighty-one engines for its new aircraft.

During the next decade improved versions were created. Seventeen foreign licences were sold for the Jupiter and over 7,100 were built, powering more than 200 different types of aircraft. Other engines included the 36hp Cherub, the Mercury rated at 960hp and the big 1,065hp Pegasus. A great advance was the sleeve-valved Hydra with sixteen small cylinders in eight pairs with a common head. It did not go into production. A series of sleeve-valve engines followed; the Perseus and Aquila, the twin-row 14-cylinder Hercules, the Taurus and finally the 2,520hp Centaurus, the last of Bristol's great family of piston engines.

Strangely, BACo seemed to ignore gas turbine engines until about 1940 when studies of propeller-turbines began. This was understandable as Fedden was totally immersed in the development of sleeve-valve piston engines for the RAF at war. However, he had been privately studying gas turbine technology. It was December 1946 before the 2,000hp Theseus turboprop was type tested. By then the 4,000hp Proteus turboprop was being prepared for the Brabazon and the Princess flying boat. Stanley Hooker had a long six-year development programme with this engine, but neither of these big aeroplanes entered production. Instead, the Proteus powered the Britannia airliner and provided millions of trouble-free flying hours. From the start the Olympus turbojet, with a design thrust of 9,140lb, was a superb power unit. It produced a full 10,000lb on its first test run in May 1950 and continuous development resulted in a thrust of 39,940lb when installed in Concorde. At the other end of the power scale was the 3,000lb thrust Orpheus which went on to deliver some 5,800lb. Thousands were produced by Bristol and licence-built in Italy, Germany and India.

The air-cooled radial Jupiter, which Bristol inherited when it acquired Cosmos Engineering along with Roy Fedden and his design team, was the first power unit to come out of the new Patchway engine works in 1922.

In 1958 Hooker's team began designing a vectored-thrust engine with swivelling jet pipes for fixed-wing vertical take-off aircraft. This became the Pegasus which powers the Harrier/Sea Harrier/Matador/AV-8A and -B family of operational VTOL aircraft.

In 1959 things changed at Filton. Bristol Aero Engines (formed in 1956) and Armstrong Siddeley Motors merged to become Bristol Siddeley Engines Ltd (BSEL) which then absorbed the de Havilland and Blackburn engine interests. Pegasus and other engines were developed and produced by BSEL until October 1966. Then, Rolls-Royce acquired BSEL for £63 million to prevent it linking up with Pratt & Whitney in the USA on the JT9D engine, the first of the giant commercial turbofans. Thus, the aero-engine plant at Filton became the Bristol Engine Division of Rolls-Royce. Thereafter, all engines being developed or in production there were continued under the world-renowned and revered 'RR' badge of the great Rolls-Royce company.

Above: *Pictured in 1942, Sir Roy Fedden with some of his original 1921 engine department staff. From left: S. Damsell, R.N. Swinchatt, ? Brown, ? Gulliford, W. Stammers, F. Powell, H. Wills, -?-, R. Williams, Fedden, ? Cox, A.G. Adams, ? Bennett, L.F. 'Bunny' Butler, A. Houlson, ? Collett, ? O'Gorman.*

Opposite
Above: *Assembling the Mercury engines clearly required a lot of skilled hands and minds. Thirty-three men are working on eighteen engines.*

Below:*The last of the great Bristol radial engines was the 18-cylinder twin-row Centaurus finally giving 2,520hp.*

An Olympus 593 engine for Concorde being prepared for test running.

A Pegasus vectored thrust engine for the Sea Harrier VTOL aircraft in the final stages of assembly at Filton in September 1983.

Dudbridge Iron Works

It was in early 1912 that this Stroud-based company obtained a licence from Emile Salmson to build his water-cooled radial aero-engines. The Salmson company had a small factory at Billancourt, Paris. These engines were quite complex as they used the patented Swiss Canton Unne system in which all the connecting rods drove a cage revolving on the crankpin on epicyclic gears. Dudbridge got back some of the money paid to Salmson by selling a sub-licence to Willans & Robinson in Rugby, one of the five companies which would form the foundations of the English Electric Co. It is believed that Dudbridge Iron Works built over 300 of these 130hp and 200hp engines some of which were fitted in British-built Maurice Farman biplanes.

Brockworth Engineering Co. Ltd

From 1937 Metropolitan Vickers Electrical Co. in Manchester had built components for an axial-flow jet engine designed by the Royal Aircraft Establishment at Farnborough. In 1940 'Metrovick' began designing and building its own engines. On 13 November 1943 one of these, designated the F.2/1, was the first British axial-flow engine to fly in a Gloster F9/40 prototype Meteor. At the war's end, having successfully developed this engine to become the F.9 version, Metrovick decided to give up making aero engines. The Ministry of Supply wanted this engine, now named Sapphire, to be further developed and, in January 1948, Armstrong Siddeley Motors (ASM), a Hawker Siddeley company, was given this work. ASM made some major changes to the design and developed the engine still further until a completely new series of Sapphire engines was created.

For the specific purpose of manufacturing this new Sapphire, Brockworth Engineering Co. Ltd, was formed by Hawker Siddeley Group in the summer 1951. It took over most of the one million square feet floor space of what had been Gloster Aircraft's shadow factory which A.W. Hawkesley had occupied for Albemarle production. In addition, engine test cells were built on the extreme end of the airfield. These engines powered the Gloster Javelin, Handley Page Victor, two Hawker Hunter variants and prototypes of the English Electric Lightning and Avro Vulcan. Later, Brockworth Engineering overhauled some Orenda engines used in the Royal Canadian Air Force's Canadian-built Sabre jet fighters based in Europe.

While this particular Sapphire Mk 104 engine never powered an aeroplane, lots of others did. This splendid sectioned engine was an eye-catching exhibit on the Hawker Siddeley stand in the 1956 Society of British Aircraft Constructors Exhibition at Farnborough.

four

The Equipment
Makers

Aircraft Components Company

Worcester-born George Herbert Dowty was a man with ideas, the ability to turn them into hardware and to sell them. He learned about aircraft engineering at the local polytechnic before working at British Aerial Transport Co. where, in 1918, he had his first encounter with aircraft design, especially undercarriages. He then joined a scientific instrument maker followed by an elevator and conveyor company, the British Portland Cement and the Dunlop Rubber companies. His next job after these was with A.V. Roe at Hamble where he claimed to be an undercarriage expert (and compared with most draughtsmen, he was). This was in 1921 and he remained there until 1924 during which time he worked on the unlovely Aldershot bomber and equally unappealing Bison naval aircraft. Dowty made his penultimate move to Gloucestershire Aircraft Co. (GAC) in Cheltenham where H.P. Folland was leading the design of the Gamecock fighter. In his never-ending efforts to achieve high performance from his fighter designs Folland paid great attention to streamlining. Young George Dowty was equally exercised about the design of contemporary undercarriage's shock-absorbing struts which stuck out into the breeze and were used only for take-off and landing. Having done some sums he discovered that they created seventeen per cent of the total drag of the aeroplane and he referred to these excrescences as 'built-in headwinds'.

In his spare time he designed some revolutionary streamlined shock-absorbing undercarriage struts, using compression rubber springing, and wrote to every British aircraft manufacturer. Not one was interested. In January 1931, using an accommodation address in the City of London and a helpful freelance office manager, he formed Aircraft Components Co. (ACCo). The only stumbling block was that he was still a GAC employee. Thus, his spare time was taken up with design work, some administration and publicising his struts through lectures to the Royal Aeronautical Society branches and articles for the weekly aviation magazines.

The first order came from Juan de la Cierva y Cordoniu, the Spanish inventor of the autogyro, one of which was being built in secret by de Havilland. Two struts were intended for this aeroplane. Now George had to make them. With the help of two GAC craftsmen, one having a foot-operated lathe in his cellar for machining and the other a large garden shed for final assembly, the struts were made and were fitted to the Cierva C.24 autogyro. It flew on 20 September 1931.

Dowty's next success was the internally-sprung wheel which contained the shock-absorbers, suspension and the brakes. With this wheel a single rigid streamlined cantilevered leg replaced the traditional multi-strutted and braced type. An article by George Dowty in *Aircraft Engineering* prompted an enquiry from the Japanese Kawasaki company who ordered six wheels. This was serious business requiring serious attention. The only way was for Dowty to quit his GAC drawing board. With his two GAC friends and help from a local garage the wheels were made in ACCo's first 'factory', which was a Cheltenham Mews loft, then shipped to Japan, with payment made while they were still only four days out from London Docks!

Other orders began to arrive; 250 Bristol Bulldog tailwheels, struts for the Airspeed Ferry and a retractable landing gear (as Dowty referred to undercarriages generally) for the

This Japanese Kawasaki KDA-5 Type 92 fighter was the first aircraft type to have Aircraft Components Co.'s internally sprung wheels.

A batch of forty-one castoring tailwheel units for Bristol Bulldog fighters ready for delivery to Filton in 1934.

Heston Phoenix. Though small, these orders required larger premises and ACCo moved on and up with a new name – Aircraft Components Ltd (ACL). Then, through the local grapevine in 1933, he learned that GAC was expecting an order for its SS.19B fighter. When 228 aircraft, now named Gauntlet, were ordered, they all had ACL landing gear struts. In September 1934 a new Gloster fighter, the Gladiator, flew with Dowty's internally-sprung wheel. During the next five years 747 Gladiators were built at Hucclecote, each with Dowty's wheels.

When George Dowty was looking for even bigger accommodation for ACL he was given financial support and advice by A.W. Martyn, chairman of H.H. Martyn & Co. in Cheltenham, and Hugh Burroughes, chairman of Gloster Aircraft Co. ACL then moved to Arle Court on the town's outskirts. It was from here that the company expanded in many different ways. This coincided with the great RAF Expansion schemes. After years of British disarmament and appeasement policies, Germany's illegal rearming and formation

George Dowty gave to H.P. Folland, free-of-charge, a set of these slender shock-absorbing landing gear legs to try out on this prototype Gauntlet. Over 200 Gauntlets with these legs were built.

This very clean landing gear on the Gladiator was made possible by the use of the Dowty internally-sprung wheels on cantilevered legs.

of the Luftwaffe had to be addressed. At Arle Court the design and manufacture of retractable landing gear and high pressure hydraulic systems moved up several gears and soon production work was being placed with sub-contractors. When war was declared on 3 September 1939 Aircraft Components Ltd was ready.

The company's contribution to the wartime aircraft industry and to the success of Royal Air Force operations was immense. In 1940 ACL became Dowty Equipment Ltd (DEL). Very few British aircraft were not Dowty-equipped. Gladiator, Hurricane, Typhoon, Whirlwind, Skua fighters; Battle, Blenheim, Halifax, Lancaster and Stirling bombers... the list goes on. History was made several times in May 1941 when the Allies' first jet aircraft, the Gloster E28/39 first flew. Its Dowty landing gear was the first tricycle type to be fitted on a Gloster aeroplane.

When peace returned in August 1945 Dowty's wartime production totalled an incredible 87,000 landing gear units and nearly a million hydraulic system components, and a new subsidiary company, Dowty Electrics, had been formed. But George Dowty was a worried man. He knew that there would be great reductions in orders for military aircraft equipment and the spectre of empty factories haunted him. However, he knew that the company had great experience in hydraulic engineering. Where could this asset be best exploited? Five war years of almost no equipment development in the coal-mining industry seemed a good target. Just a year later the first set of Dowty hydraulic pit props went underground to replace traditional wooden props and bars. There is a story that their speedy development was due to the fact that, in essence, their design was one half of a Lancaster main landing gear!

But there was a great upsurge in work in the new field of fuel-system design and engineering. With encouragement from de Havilland it appeared that there could be a good future for work of this kind. Personnel and facilities were gathered, system components were produced and test flown on the new DH engine, the Ghost, which was proven in the DH Comet four-jet airliner. Soon other jet engine manufacturers were knocking on Dowty's door.

The Cold War and the Korean War created an ongoing need for new military aircraft. New British civil aircraft projects were coming into fruition including the Bristol Brabazon,

The Bristol Britannia's British Messier nose landing gear, here being admired at the 1952 SBAC Exhibition at Farnborough, was one of several produced by BM which became part of the Dowty Rotol range of products.

a giant transatlantic airliner for which Dowty provided the enormous landing gear. Soon after it first flew on 4 September 1949 another new Dowty company, Dowty Seals Ltd, opened for business. Originally launched to serve aircraft hydraulics, through cross-fertilisation of polymer-based technologies it produced many industrial products too.

The year 1956 was milestone year for Dowty, the company and the man. In June the company celebrated its Silver Jubilee and George became Sir George Dowty for his outstanding services to the aircraft industry.

In 1958 Bristol Aeroplane's Dr Stanley Hooker was beginning to design the first vectored-thrust engine for vertical take-off and landing aircraft. This was the Pegasus which first ran at Bristol in September 1959 with a DFS fuel control system. It was ten years before the production engine entered RAF service in the Harrier GR.1 in April 1969. Large numbers of Pegasus engines with ever-increasing power were built and flew with Dowty fuel control systems.

The amalgamation of Dowty Equipment Ltd with Rotol Airscrews Ltd on 1 April 1960 was a big advance for both companies. Located at Staverton, a couple of miles from Arle Court, Rotol had been owned jointly by Rolls-Royce and Bristol Aeroplane Co. and earlier had acquired British Messier, also at Staverton, which made landing gear and hydraulic systems. This marriage of a company which made things which went round and round with one which made things which went up and down, was to create the powerhouse of Dowty's aerospace endeavours in later years. It was named Dowty Rotol Ltd (DRL).

Whenever possible, George Dowty was always keen to display his company's products in international exhibitions. The 1967 Paris Air Show was of great historical and commercial significance to Dowty. At Le Bourget Robert Hunt, Dowty's deputy chairman, and René Lucien, president of Messier SA signed an agreement to form two joint companies, Dowty Messier Ltd and Messier Dowty SARL with the aim of supplying equipment to Anglo-French and other aerospace programmes.

Then, following a long period of illness, Sir George Dowty died on 7 December 1975. Since its inception he had been the mainspring driving the majority of the company's endeavours. Typically, he had worked until two days before his death. He was succeeded by Robert Hunt who had been one of his first pair of apprentices in May 1935.

A collaborative programme by DRL and the Aircraft Research Association produced a new family of propeller blade aerofoil sections which were used on DRL's advanced technology propellers. Another bit of ground-breaking technology was the use of composite materials for propeller blades. These have carbon-fibre spars with moulded outer shells having the new aerofoil sections and filled with polyurethane foam. A unique event was recorded on 10 June 1977 when a twin-engined Britten-Norman Islander first flew with a new quiet aircraft propulsion unit. This was the DRL ducted propulsor comprising a variable-pitch multi-bladed fan rotating inside a close-fitting cowling. In 1978 all Dowty aviation companies were grouped together in a new Aviation and Defence Division. The following year Robert Hunt, Dowty Group chairman was created a Knight for his services to the aviation industry and to the community.

The year 1977 saw two significant events in the Dowty story. In the spring, Dowty acquired Ultra Electronic Holdings which signalled a growing emphasis on things electronic. An exciting venture was announced on 4 November when a new company

November 1960. The Hawker P.1127 Harrier prototype vertical take-off aircraft with its unusual Dowty 'bicycle' landing gear and wing-tip balancing wheels.

Dowty and Smiths Industries Controls (DSIC) was formed by the two companies jointly to exploit their individual special skills in fuel control systems technology.

In 1980 the Government began modest funding of a full–authority digital electronic control (FADEC) the supplier being DSIC. The Pegasus was one of the world's very early engines to fly with such a superior control system which, among other benefits, provided absolute precision in engine control and found its own faults.

The 1980s were a buoyant period for Dowty aviation companies exemplified by a February 1984 announcement by the Fokker organisation in the Netherlands regarding its F.27 Friendship short-haul transport aircraft equipped with Dowty landing gear, propellers and electrics. The type had logged 11 million landings, 10 million flying hours in service with 177 airlines, Governments and other operators in 62 countries. When the last propeller for use on the Dart engine was delivered in April 1986, so ended a production run of over 6,500 propellers during a thirty-year period. In the same year the first Harrier II GR5 flew with a DSIC digital engine control system for the first time.

The break up of Dowty Group was foreshadowed in 1989 with the management buy-outs of the mining and industrial hydraulics businesses. There were top management changes and then, in June 1992, the TI Group made a successful bid for Dowty Group's aerospace, polymer, electronics, and communications businesses, eventually disposing of the last two. These Dowty Group aerospace companies formed one of TI's four group businesses. In 1993 Dowty Fuel Systems was sold to Lucas, and the TI Group and SNECMA in France merged their landing gear interests in Messier-Dowty International to form the leading world-class landing gear business with a multi-million pound investment in new facilities at Staverton. Finally, SNECMA bought TI's half share in Messier-Dowty International. In addition to landing gear for a number of military aircraft, including the Jaguar, Tornado and Eurofighter Typhoon, the company produces landing gear for all of the current Airbus variants.

Sir George Dowty with Hawker Aircraft's renowned test pilot Squadron Leader Neville Duke, who later flew the Dowty Group's DH Dove business aircraft.

Rotol Airscrews Ltd

On page 63 reference was made to Dr Hele-Shaw, Tom Beacham and Harry 'Pop' Milner who were designing and building variable-pitch propellers. The complex negotiations in the corridors of power in the Air Ministry, Bristol Aeroplane Co. and Gloster Aircraft concerning the subject of variable-pitch propellers are not for these pages; suffice it to say that in May 1937 Rolls-Royce, and Bristol, formed a joint company to manufacture propellers of this type. Its name was formed from the first two letters and the last three letters of their respective names: Rotol Airscrews Ltd.

The place chosen for this company's factory was Staverton, conveniently located not only between Bristol and Derby, which was Rolls-Royce's main factory, but between Gloucester and Cheltenham; it was also close to the new airport. But first the Cotswold Aero Club had to be persuaded to move to an adjacent site on the airport before building work could begin. This progressed rapidly and the first Rotol airscrew with wooden blades was delivered to Farnborough for testing in December 1937. Finding the best material for airscrew blades was an ongoing task with pressed wood, Duralumin and magnesium being investigated.

When first established Rotol's rate of production was set at 10 airscrews per week but as the RAF's Expansion schemes gathered momentum this was raised to 100 per week. With the outbreak of war in September 1939, this weekly target was increased to 150. Apart from

A Gloster Grebe with a Hele-Shaw Beacham constant-speed two-bladed variable-pitch propeller being flight tested at Hucclecote in 1928.

Rotol's Hawker Tornado prototype, R7936, at Staverton for lengthy trials of a six-bladed contra-prop in September 1941.

the production and development of airscrews their flight testing was an all-important facet of the company's responsibilities. In 1939 a Flight Test Department was established at the airfield close to the main factory. However, with the threat of air attack in mind, dispersal of various design and production departments was in hand. In addition to airscrews Rotol also produced a range of auxiliary gearboxes for a variety of installations.

During the war several different types of airscrews were developed; feathering and non-feathering, electrically and hydraulically operated and with three, four or five wood or metal blades. It was not until the latter war years that the contra-rotating propeller appeared having two banks of three blades rotating in opposite directions. A multi-bladed fan, designed for fitting to Bristol Hercules radial engines for improved cooling, was designed and built in quantity by Rotol's dispersed factory in Scotland.

In October 1943 the name of the company was changed to Rotol Limited. The official reason was that as Rotol now had a range of aviation products, the 'Airscrews' should be dropped. There is, however, a possibly apocryphal story that an RAF bomber squadron, which had lost a number of pilots and crews in a particularly hazardous operation, had telephoned a training unit to provide six complete aircrews as soon as possible. The next morning a Queen Mary articulated vehicle rolled up to the squadron with half a dozen neatly crated airscrews! After that, it was said, airscrews were called 'propellers' again.

This company name-change coincided with the unveiling of another product. This was a range of small sleeve-valve engines, one of which, a 60hp unit, was used as an Auxiliary Generating Plant to provide current for aircraft services. However, when its misuse in a prototype flying boat caused it to set this aircraft on fire and totally destroy it, this AGP disappeared. Only about fifty of some smaller versions were produced. It is, perhaps, not totally surprising that, with a wealth of knowledge about variable pitch airscrews, Rotol should turn its attention to marine screws. What *is* surprising, however, is that it had sufficient design and manufacturing capacity to undertake this work in 1941. In the event, a large range of different marine craft were equipped with Rotol variable-pitch screws and manufacturing continued into the 1950s.

When peace returned in 1945 there were many changes at Rotol, in personnel, in production facilities and in markets. During the war years Rotol had produced 100,000 propellers for over sixty different types of aircraft and many different engines. This was an incredible effort for a new company. Now the future was uncertain. Would the jet engine put the propeller out of business? Would the market for light aircraft propellers be big enough? The questions were many, and all difficult. But work on propellers and auxiliary gearboxes continued at a slower rate.

Rotol six-bladed contra-rotating propellers on the Brabazon during early engine-running trials at Filton in 1949.

Like all the 460 Vickers Viscount airliners which were produced, the four Rolls-Royce Dart turbo-prop engines in this Air France Viscount turned Rotol four-bladed propellers.

Among the early post-war aircraft to have Rotol propellers was the Bristol Brabazon; its eight radial engines mounted in coupled pairs drove six 16ft diameter co-axial metal-bladed propellers. Contra-rotating and co-axial propellers where each propeller had its own engine, were built for the Fairey Gannet. Perhaps the most rewarding aeroplane from Rotol's point of view was the splendid Vickers Viscount airliner of which 460 were built. Each was powered by four Rolls-Royce Dart turboprops which turned Rotol propellers. Ancillary equipment included electrics, feathering pumps, governor units, synchronisers and gearboxes. Quite a rewarding package.

In 1949 Rotol acquired British Messier, an aircraft hydraulics and landing gear company, buying Bristol Aeroplane Co.'s fifty per cent holding and the other fifty per cent from Arbo Investments.

By the late 1950s the lack of new aviation orders was worrying and Rotol was looking for non-aviation products to keep the factory busy. It was in 1957 that there were rumours of talks with the Dowty company regarding a take-over but this was not confirmed until December 1958. The merger officially took place on 1 April 1960. The Rotol story thereafter is that of Dowty Rotol.

British Messier Limited

Louis Silvio Armandias arrived in England from France in 1936. He brought with him a licence from the French company Messier to enable him to produce its products in the UK. His first order was for the landing gear and hydraulics for a Handley Page aeroplane which became the Halifax four-engined bomber. With the Rubery Owen company and its Warrington factory which manufactured this equipment, he formed Rubery Owen Messier. After quitting this company he experienced some exciting and eventful war years. Then in 1947 he helped to launch British Messier Ltd with Bristol Aeroplane Co. holding fifty per cent and Arbo Investments the other half. It began life in a clutch of wooden sheds at one end of the site occupied by Rotol Limited at Staverton. There, Armandias, who was now managing director, gathered a young but skilful team of design engineers. An early order was for hydraulic jacks to operate the Canberra jet bomber's air brakes. Once again a Messier company had to sub-contract the production of its designs and this work was done by Rotol.

In 1949, as recorded earlier, Rotol Limited bought British Messier from Bristol Aeroplane Co. and Arbro Investments and became a wholly-owned Rotol subsidiary. The Bristol Britannia's landing gear was a challenging project but it emerged as a stylish, well-engineered product for this elegant airliner. With the Dowty acquisition of Rotol Ltd in 1959 very soon the name British Messier was supplanted on products by Rotol.

S. Smith & Sons

The origins of the Smiths company date back to 1851 when Samuel Smith opened a small business to make and sell watches and clocks in Newington Causeway near the Elephant & Castle in London. His son, also Samuel Smith, inherited this prosperous business and, in 1873, opened larger premises in the Strand with other shops being opened later in Piccadilly and Trafalgar Square. With the advent of the motor car, in 1904 young Samuel added 'motor watches' and speedometers to his range of products. Three years later the business received its first Royal Warrant having supplied the speedometers in cars for His Royal Highness the Prince of Wales. As the production of motor accessories grew, ten years later S. Smith & Sons (Motor Accessories) Ltd was formed to develop this side of the business under the direction of Gordon Smith, Samuel Smith Junior's son.

It was in 1911 that the first aviation instrument was made. This was an engine revolution indicator for the Mercury monoplane built by young Robert Blackburn in Leeds.

When war came in 1914 there was an urgent need for Smiths' products and the following year a new factory was built at Cricklewood to handle the explosive growth and ever-widening range of military vehicle and aviation products. At the war's end Smiths was advertising a complete aviation instrument panel with Imperial or Metric units. Then, when Alcock and Brown made their first non-stop flight across the Atlantic in 1919, their Vickers Vimy had Smiths instrumentation. To further augment the product range, in 1927 the British Jaeger instrument company and the renowned spark plug manufacturer KLG joined the Smiths organisation (KLG were the initials of its founder, the well-known racing

From a single shop in London, S. Smith & Son's business grew with three more being opened. This one, in the Strand, was pictured in 1873. They were the forerunners of the great Smiths Industries Group.

driver Kenelm Lee Guinness, who could not obtain sparking plugs able to survive the very high temperatures in racing-car engines. In 1912 he began designing and producing his own plugs. Their high quality was soon recognised by the motor car and aviation industries and this small venture, which began in the cellar of an old coaching inn near Kingston-on-Thames, rapidly grew into a major company). 1927 also saw Great Britain win the Schneider Trophy Contest with the Supermarine S5 racing floatplane which had Smiths instrumentation and its Napier Lion engine used KLG spark plugs. In the cockpit was Flt Lt Stanley Norman Webster, a member of the RAF High Speed Flight. Twenty-three years later Air Vice Marshal S.N. Webster was to join Smiths as area manager at its Cheltenham factory. But that was the future.

It was a prescient observation by the Ministry of Aircraft Production in January 1939 which added to Gloucestershire's tally of aviation companies. At a meeting with Smiths management, Ministry moguls pointed out that their factory on the North Circular Road at Cricklewood, North London, would be very vulnerable to air attack in any future war. This was only three months after Prime Minister Neville Chamberlain, returning from the last of several meetings with Adolf Hitler, had stepped out of a British Airways Lockheed 14 aircraft at Heston triumphantly waving a small piece of paper. Referring to it later that day, he said 'I believe that this means peace in our time'. Sadly, it was not to be. But Smiths took notice of the MAP's warning and sought a new site in the West Country far from Cricklewood.

In April an area of land at Bishops Cleeve near Cheltenham was acquired and work began on building a new factory for a Smiths subsidiary company S. Smith & Sons (Cheltenham) Ltd. which was formed on 6 July. This factory opened in May 1940. Just three months later, as the Ministry had feared, Cricklewood was bombed. But why had Bishops Cleeve been chosen from among the sites visited? The legend has it that when Sir Allan Gordon-Smith, Smiths' managing director and a keen horse-racing man, learned of its proximity to Cheltenham Racecourse, it seemed to be exactly the right place. Another attraction was the flat land adjacent to the site which could be used by the Percival Vega Gull which was the company's demonstration and communications aircraft.

Back in 1931 Smiths had patented a pneumatic automatic pilot and, later, had seen it being installed in the majority of the RAF's heavy bomber force where it was universally-known as 'George'. Smiths then developed its first all-electric autopilot which was first demonstrated at the 1947 Society of British Aircraft Constructors Exhibition and Display at Handley Page's Radlett airfield.

The earliest known installation of a Smiths instrument in an aircraft was the engine revolution indicator in a Blackburn Mercury monoplane in 1911.

The bubble sextant was among Smiths aircraft equipment produced during the Second World War. This Wellington bomber's navigator occupies the fuselage-top astrodome to use his sextant.

Bishops Cleeve 1961. Autopilot gyros being assembled in Smiths Clean Room which maintained almost surgical cleanliness.

An important element of Smiths' development facilities was the Flying Unit which, over the years, operated a wide range of aircraft. Starting in 1935 with a DH Dragon, it was followed by the Vega Gull which was impressed into RAF service during the war. Based at Staverton from 1945, the Unit's Percival Proctor was used until 1947 when an Avro XIX – a civilian Anson in effect – also joined the Flight. For a time a Ministry of Supply Vickers Varsity was flown from Gloster's Moreton Valence airfield in collaboration with Rotol which had a Lancaster operating from there. Then there was a little Miles Gemini before a Dakota, DH Dove and, at different times, two Vickers Varsities joined the Unit. These aircraft were used to develop a range of flight systems including the Para-Visual Director and the amazing Autoland system. One Varsity made more than 700 fully automatic landings in the Autoland development programme. Before the Unit was closed in October 1969 an Avro 748 had been added to the fleet. Today, powerful computers in the design laboratories simulate aircraft so precisely that most of the development and trials work is carried out on the ground rather than in the air.

During the 1950s Smiths' 3,000 employees were beavering away on flight deck instruments, autopilots and landing systems for all of Britain's large civil and military aeroplanes. They included the Comet and Britannia, the three V-bombers – Valiant, Vulcan and Victor – the Argosy and the Trident. Then, on a foggy 4 November 1964 when the visibility was down to fifty yards at Heathrow Airport and even the birds were walking, a

15 November 1964 at Heathrow Airport a British European Airways Trident makes the world's first automatic landing in 50 yards visibility using Smith's Autoland System.

In 1961 Smiths first supplied a mach-meter for Boeing's three-engined 727 airliner. A total of 1,500 of these aircraft were built.

British European Airways Trident made the world's first landing at a public airport in these weather conditions under the full automatic control of Smiths' Autoland system. The national daily newspapers' headlines were ecstatic: 'History comes down in the fog', 'Robot pilot lands 'blind' in the fog' and 'A no-hands landing beats the gloom'. There is a story that, in some exuberant sales conference when Autoland's accuracy was being extolled, it was claimed that the *real* reason for the Trident's nose-wheel being off-set to port was not to provide more usable space in the nose but to prevent the wheel bumping along the runway's centre-line lights when this very accurate Autoland system was being used!

With Autoland, Britain led the world in blind landing techniques with BEA later becoming the only airline to continue flying in minimum-visibility conditions. The creation of this system stemmed from the need to enable the RAF's nuclear deterrent Vulcan and Victor bombers to operate in all weathers and be a credible element of Britain's round-the-clock everyday air strike force.

Boeing 737 twin-jet short-haul airliners are equipped with Smiths combined mach-meter, standby altimeter and airspeed indicator, rate of climb meter, primary engine display and full flight auto-throttle system.

During the 1960s and onward, as Britain's aerospace industry slowly downsized the word 'Exports' was on everyone's lips. It quickly became clear that Seattle, the home of the giant Boeing company, was the place to be. Smiths were soon there; first with a mach-meter being supplied for the Boeing 727 in 1961 and six years later a combined mach-meter and airspeed indicator for the Boeing 737. These were the beginning of great things.

Propellers and landing gear are readily recognised for what they are and what they do. Smiths Aviation' products are something else. Succinctly described they are unimaginably complex devices which do unimaginable things with unimaginable reliability and precision while buried deep in the airframes and engines which get all the plaudits and glory. But it was these very elements which attracted business from around the world. Not only Boeing but many others continue to beat a path to Bishops Cleeve to buy precision instruments and controls.

The mid-1960s were all Concorde and its Olympus engines. Because of the wide operating envelope of these magnificent power units, very precise fuel and temperature control with highly accurate engine instruments were essential. In response Smiths devised a new type of instrument mechanism for Concorde, derivatives of which were later used on the big Boeing 747.

In 1977 it was Boeing 747 equipment, then the complete auto-throttle system for the 737 two years later. Smiths also started to design Integrated Circuits, or 'chips' as we now call them, at Bishops Cleeve, and with them built miniaturised self-contained digital computers. Out of this in 1979 came the world's first digital autopilot for commercial use. This was the SEP.10 which, first demonstrated in a British Aerospace Jetstream, had convinced Boeing that Smiths were clever enough to develop the 737's auto-throttle.

In 1984, when certain sections of the US aerospace industry would only buy from on-shore suppliers, Smiths bought Lear Siegler's Michigan and New Jersey businesses. Their joint skills and experience with Airbus and Boeing made Smiths world leaders in Flight Management Systems. In parallel with this Smiths tackled the task of finding a substitute for the veritable spiders-web of wires connecting the many computers and other bits of

An early export order for Smiths Head-Up-Displays came in 1973 from Sweden to equip the mighty Saab Viggen attack aircraft.

Derivatives of Smiths highly accurate engine instruments for the Concorde programme, with specially-devised mechanisms, are supplied for the Boeing 747.

electrickery in military aircraft. The answer was the Digital Data Bus which hugely reduced wiring weight and volume and increased aircraft reliability and damage tolerance. When McDonnell Douglas turned toward Bishops Cleeve with an electrical power distribution problem on the Apache helicopter, Smiths solved it by inventing and developing a compact Electrical Power Distribution System using digital computing, digital data buses and solid state power switches to replace old style relays. The same principles have been used by Smiths to control power distribution in the Boeing 777 and to control the airframe systems in the Eurofighter Typhoon.

The most recent new name among Gloucestershire aviation companies is Smiths Aerospace, created when Smiths Industries and TI Group merged in 2001, bringing together the aerospace businesses of Smiths and Dowty. In addition to Dowty Propellers, another Gloucestershire Dowty element, the high-pressure hydraulics systems and actuation businesses combine in Smiths Aerospace Actuation Systems to produce high-pressure systems and actuators for many aerospace applications. With 12,000 employees divided equally between Europe and North America, Smiths Aerospace still retains an important part of its operations in Gloucestershire.

As part of Smiths Aerospace Actuation Systems, Dowty Propellers continues to exploit the results of research and development work undertaken by Dowty Rotol in the fields of composite propeller blades and its family of new blade sections. One of the production processes is performed by a semi-automatic machine designed by Dowty Propellers which braids the moulded blade's composite fibres. Other ongoing research programmes include marine screws with composite blades.

Among the current aircraft equipped with these propellers are the US-built four-engined C-130J Hercules transport which has six-bladed propellers, Italy's C-27J Spartan twin-engined transport, Sweden's Saab 340 (the world's first aircraft to have all-composite propeller blades), the Saab 2000 passenger aircraft and the Canadian Dash 8-400 regional passenger aircraft. In addition, ducted fans with composite blades are fitted to military air-cushion vehicles in use by the US Marine Corps and US Navy.

The US Navy T-45A Goshawk, a derivative of the British Aerospace Hawk trainer, has a Smiths Head-Up Display.

Two Dowty & Smiths Industries Co. engineers set up the Full Authority Digital Electronic Control unit on this Bristol Siddeley Pegasus vectored-thrust engine prior to test running.

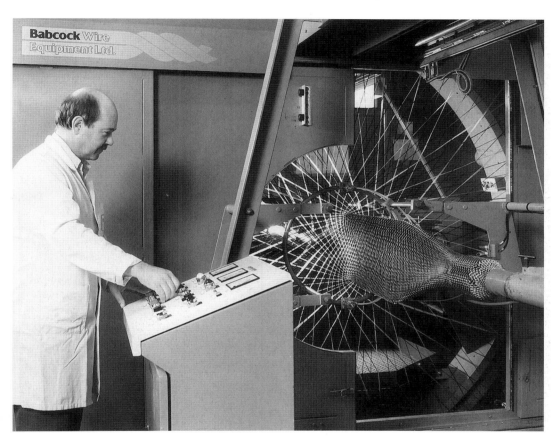

A Dowty Propellers operator monitors this semi-automatic machine which braids composite propeller blade fibres.

Above: *The US Navy's Grumman Tracker anti-submarine aircraft flies with Dowty composite bladed propellers.*

Opposite
Above: *Dowty Propellers advanced six-bladed composite propeller on the Lockheed C-130J Hercules military transport aircraft.*

Below: *The Saab 340 medium-range passenger aircraft was the first to have composite-bladed propellers.*

Ultra Electronics

The original Ultra company was formed in the 1930s and made wireless equipment before moving on to black and white television. Later still it became involved with aviation equipment, designing and manufacturing the engine controls for the Bristol Olympus engines intended for the ill-fated TSR.2 but which were developed for Concorde.

Ultra Electronics was formed in 1993 as a management buy-out from the TI Group after it had acquired Dowty Group. Ultra's Precision Air Systems company at Staverton designs and manufactures the HiPPAG high-pressure pure-air generator. This is an airborne compressor which replaces older-style rechargeable compressed-air bottles by providing a constant flow of clean air. One application is cooling sensors on heat-seeking missiles carried by the AV-8B Harrier, US AH-1 Cobra helicopter and the Super Hornet US Navy fighter. Ultra Electrics Division in Cheltenham supplies a wide range of electro–mechanical components and equipment for aircraft cockpits and control systems. Its electrical conduit systems protect the wiring harness on Messier-Dowty landing gear.

five

Royal Air Force Units and Airfields

With the inauguration of the Royal Flying Corps and its Naval Wing on 13 May 1912, small airfields began to sprout in many parts of the UK. Gloucestershire was no exception and over the years no less than twenty-six RAF airfields were located in the county, several continuing to be used today. During the 1930s the Fine Arts Commission and the Council for the Preservation of Rural England were asked to advise on the design of buildings on military airfields. They stipulated that, as far as possible, these massive creations should not harm the countryside. Thus, the buildings on the larger permanent airfields were examples of British architecture at its best. This was seen, and still is, not only by the headquarters and messes where their Georgian style blended with the rural setting, but also the hangars and workshops as well. RAF Little Rissington, the home of the Central Flying School for many years, is a classic example of this care for the environment.

In addition to the airfields, the RAF's presence in Gloucestershire included No.21 Wing HQ Royal Flying Corps which was established at Filton in August 1916 and moved to Cirencester the following month; No.7 Maintenance Unit (MU) formed in April 1939 at Quedgeley as a Universal Equipment Depot; No.59 MU formed at Newland, near Coleford as an Air Ammunition Park in May 1941; No.238 MU was established in Tewkesbury in April 1943 as a Marine Craft Servicing Unit; at Avening near Nailsworth a No.81 Group unit opened in December 1941 to control Fighter Command's Operational Training Units; No.7 Radio Maintenance Unit formed in July 1940 at Filton and then moved to Henbury; in July 1918 No.8 School of Instruction formed in Cheltenham; and No.52 Maintenance Wing reformed in May 1941 at Gatcombe Park. A records office, air traffic control unit and meteorological office occupied sites in Barnwood, Gloucester. No.24 Royal Observer Corps' operational centre was in Gloucester. All have moved, leaving the Headquarters of the Personnel Management and Training Centre at RAF Innsworth as the county's principal RAF station. Bristol University Air Squadron was formed at Filton in February 1941 and is still based there. One should not forget the Air Training Corps (originally Air Defence Cadet Corps) and its work with the youth of the county. Currently there are sixteen squadrons and two detached flights operational in Gloucestershire. No.637 (Volunteer) Gliding School used by the ATC and Combined Cadet Force is located at RAF Little Rissington.

During the Second World War seven enemy aircraft were shot down within the county.

Aston Down

6 miles SE of Stroud

Originally a First World War airfield named Minchinhampton used by two training squadrons of the Australian Flying Corps, this No.1 airfield had a variety of aircraft; Bristol Pups and Scouts followed by DH.6s, Camels, Avro 504s and Snipes. It became farm land again in 1920. Renamed Aston Down it reopened on 12 October 1938 but was substantially larger than the first field with large areas of land being requisitioned. No.20 Maintenance Unit (MU) was the first to occupy this airfield; however, a feature of all these airfields was the ever-changing list of units based at them and their differing roles. While

Minchinhampton, (renamed Aston Down in 1938) was home to Australian Flying Corps training squadrons in the First World War. Here an Avro 504K fuselage is towed from a canvas Bessoneaux hangar.

the MU remained at Aston Down for some twenty years, the airfield was home to eight different flying training units equipped with twelve or more different types of aircraft. These included Gladiators, Hurricanes, Spitfires, and Blenheims. In 1943 Gloster Aircraft had problems with the supply of Sabre engines for the Typhoon fighters being built at Hucclecote. Completed aircraft were flown to Aston Down, their engines and propellers were removed, taken by road to Hucclecote and installed in a new airframe which was then flown to Aston Down. These 'ferrying' Sabres were known as 'slave engines'. At the war's end large numbers of aircraft flew in to Aston Down for scrapping. In 1946 a Ferry Pool Training Flight was formed and remained until 1952-53. The MU closed in September 1960 and Aston Down became a Relief Landing Ground (RLG) for the RAF Central Flying School at Little Rissington until early 1976. The very active Cotswold Gliding Club is based at this airfield.

Babdown Farm

3 miles SW of Nailsworth

The quaint name of this airfield stems from the farm which provided most of the land for it. It opened in July 1940 as a Relief Landing Ground for Hullavington's No.9 Flying Training School and was first used for night flying by Harts and Audaxes. A month later it's was attacked by a single German bomber and a similar attack was made in March 1941. Babdown was used by a Flying Instructors' School and in June a Beam Approach Training Flight moved in and future bomber pilots practised their blind-approach flying there. Later French Navy pilots and their Ansons were based there and after the war No.7 MU at Quedgeley took over some of the hangars for storage purposes. The airfield was then returned for farming again.

Miles Master trainers were flown by No.3 Flying Instructors School at Babdown Farm during 1942-43.

Barnsley Park

4 miles NE of Cirencester

Part of an estate near Cirencester, it opened in June 1941 as a Satellite Landing Ground for No.6 MU at Brize Norton. It was closed until September 1942 when No.5 MU at Kemble took it over, but it was November 1943 before some Hurricanes moved in. Large numbers of aircraft arrived in 1944 and in September 1945 this SLG closed. When a large area of steel mesh used as taxi-ways and strips was removed it was handed back for farming.

Bibury

6 miles NE of Cirencester

This site, known as Bibury Camp, was earmarked in April 1939 as a potential landing ground, and by April 1940 No.3 Service Flying Training School's (SFTS) Oxford trainers were regular visitors. During the autumn of 1940, Bibury was the base for operations by No.87 Squadron's Hurricanes and No.92 Squadron's Spitfires which formed part of the air defences of the West of England. On 19 August, just hours after the Spitfires had landed, the airfield was attacked by a Junkers 88 dive-bomber. Two Spitfires gave chase and finally destroyed the enemy aircraft over the Solent. The SFTS returned when the fighters left at the end of 1941. Then the Beam Approach Training Flight arrived during summer 1943. Further development of the airfield included the laying of the two Sommerfeld metal runways and the erection of additional hangars. By the end of 1944 all flying had ended, Bibury was taken over by No.7 MU who used it until the airfield closed the following year.

Blakehill Farm

8 miles NE of Malmesbury

Another airfield located on a farm, this one was not built until 1943 and became an RAF Transport Command station with special roadways for moving Horsa gliders. In early March 1944 No.233 Squadron's Dakotas flew in, followed by the HQ Wing of the Glider Pilot Regiment. Then on 26 and 30 March, first the 13th Parachute Company then the 1st Canadian Parachute Company arrived. There was much to-ing and fro-ing as different units arrived, exercised, then left and more Dakotas and Horsas were gathered up. On 25 and 26 April three of No.233 Squadron's Dakotas dropped leaflets on Caen in preparation for 'things to come'. Training was focussed on accuracy in paratroop drops and large-scale glider exercises. Finally, at 22.50hrs on 5 June, take-offs began with six Dakotas towing troop-carrying Horsas followed by twenty-four Dakotas packed with paratroops. Supply drops were carried out the next night. On 13 June two No.233 Squadron's Dakotas made the first Transport Command landings in France after D-Day and returned with the first air evacuated casualties. From then on there were five daily supply flights with casualties and other personnel carried on return flights. By September Blakehill Farm's Dakota fleet had doubled in size and No.437 Squadron (Royal Canadian Air Force) began forming in preparation for the Arnhem operation. For the initial assault Dakota and Horsa pairings delivered over 450 troops as part of the ill-fated operations against Arnhem, Eindhoven and Nijmegen between 17-26 September 1944. At least eight of Blakehill's Dakotas were lost.

In May 1945 Blakehill Farm's two 'resident squadrons' moved away and No.22 Heavy Glider Conversion Unit arrived with US Hadrian gliders towed by Albemarles. A number of other squadrons and units arrived and left with the last Dakota leaving on 29 January 1946 when RAF Training Command took control of this station.

Brockworth

4 miles SE of Gloucester

For the great majority of its operational life Brockworth airfield belonged to Gloucestershire/Gloster Aircraft Co. It originated in 1915 as an Air Board Aircraft Acceptance Park to handle the aircraft being built by H.H. Martyn & Co. in Cheltenham. In 1918 the 140-acre Park had thirty buildings of different sizes covering some 20 acres.

It is recorded that there were 350 military and civilian staff. No.90 Squadron RFC was there for a time in July 1918 and No.86 Squadron began to reform there during October, but with the ending of the war in November this was abandoned. For sometime thereafter Brockworth was a No.7 Group storage unit.

In 1921 Gloucestershire Aircraft Co. rented a hangar on the airfield to house its aircraft. It gradually occupied more rented space until it bought the whole site for £15,000. This airfield was used by Gloster Aircraft until 1963 when it became a trading estate. Other companies using Brockworth during the Second World War were A.W. Hawkesley who built the Albemarle and Short Brothers who built a number of Stirlings there when Shorts factories at Rochester and Belfast were devastated by enemy air attacks in August 1940.

Brockworth airfield 1955. Gloster's Hucclecote factory occupies the foreground. The 1917 Aircraft Acceptance Park buildings are extreme top left. No.2 Shadow Factory is the black building beyond.

Chedworth

8 miles N of Cirencester

This airfield was opened in April 1942 and almost immediately was used by No.52 Operational Conversion Unit with Spitfires and Master trainers. A training unit for future leaders of Fighter Command's squadrons was opened in January 1943 but soon moved away to make room for the Oxfords from No.3 Advanced Flying Unit (AFU) at South Cerney where their airfield was waterlogged. In October air gunnery sections of Nos 60 and 63 OTUs arrived with Mosquitos and Martinet target tugs. They stayed until January 1944 when No.3 AFU returned. Then, during June–July the 125th Liaison Squadron, USAAF, with little L-5 Sentinel aircraft, operated from Chedworth. These were followed by Mustangs belonging to C Squadron of No.3 Tactical Exercise Unit (TEU) based at Aston Down. This TEU was reformed as No.55 Operational Training Unit which arrived in December 1944 flying Typhoons for fighter-bombing training. This ended in about June 1945 and Chedworth was empty until December when the Admiralty used it for storage. Thereafter the Central Flying School aircraft used it for forced-landing practice and as late as 1977 Chedworth saw RAF Wessex helicopters operating there. By then most of the airfield had become farm land again.

Down Ampney

6 miles SE of Cirencester

Nos 48 and 271 Squadrons were the first to arrive in February 1944 with Dakota transport aircraft and they were followed by their Horsa gliders and specialist ground personnel. For the next three months these squadrons took part in a great training programme with other squadrons which were to prepare them for their part in Operation *Overlord*, the Allied invasion of France on 6 June 1944. During the night 5/6 June forty-six Dakotas, some towing gliders but most carrying paratroops, were airborne by 23.20hrs and delivered them to their designated drop zone in Normandy. Late on the following day thirty-seven Horsa gliders with troops were towed to the fighting area and in darkness on 7 June the Dakotas took part in a large operation to drop supplies to the ground forces. During the next three months Down Ampney's Dakotas continued to deliver personnel and supplies on outward flights, returning with those wounded in the battles. By the end of August more than 20,000 wounded had been flown home. But there was little respite for the squadrons.

On 17 September, as part of the initial airborne assault on Arnhem, forty-nine Dakotas towing gliders took-off for Holland. A supplies mission with a similar number of aircraft was flown the next two days. By then the enemy had increased its anti-aircraft defences and among the several Dakotas which were shot down was a No.271 Squadron aircraft flown by Flight Lieutenant David Lord. Although his aircraft was badly damaged by ground fire and had one engine in flames he checked to see that none of his crew were injured. He decided to make for the drop zone where almost all of the vital supply containers were released. Lord then ordered his crew to bale out, but before all were clear he could no longer control the aircraft and it crashed in flames. There was only one survivor. In recognition of his brave action Flt Lt Lord was awarded a posthumous Victoria Cross.

Throughout the remainder of that year and early 1945 many of Down Ampney's Dakotas continued to bring back casualties from across the Channel. However, in March a large number of aircraft moved to Gosfield, Essex from where they towed Horsas in the Rhine-crossing airlift operation. Before the year's end, two Royal Canadian Air Force Dakota squadrons moved in replacing No.48 Squadron. They continued making cross-Channel flights until early 1946 when they returned home and the airfield was released.

Down Farm

3 miles SW of Tetbury

This airfield, No.23 Satellite Landing Ground, became a highly effective aircraft storage and dispersal site. Allocated to No.10 MU Hullavington, it opened in April 1941 and received a few Defiant fighters and Hampden bombers. Plans were put in hand to build a large US Army Air Force base here but these were cancelled. Although Down Farm had no runways, only grass strips, the land was deemed fit to accept four-engined heavy bombers but Sommerfeld metal tracking was laid down in 1943. Large numbers of aircraft arrived during 1944. This airfield also was used by an Advanced Flying Unit which carried out night flying and circuit training with Oxford trainers in March 1945. With the end of the war in Europe even greater numbers of aircraft were stored here. By the end of January 1946 they had all left and when some 150 tons of Sommerfeld tracking had been removed the airfield became farmland again.

Fairford

8 miles E of Cirencester

Although Fairford is often associated only with the US Air Force and the Royal International Air Tattoo, when this airfield was opened in January 1944 it was as an RAF Bomber Command station. Two months later it became part of 38 Group Transport Command with two squadrons of Stirling IVs arriving. They were followed by large numbers of Horsa gliders which, towed by the Stirlings, began day and night exercises. At midnight on 5 June 1944, forty-five Stirlings, carrying nearly 900 paratroops, began taking-off to participate in Operation *Overlord,* the D-Day landings in Normandy. On their return to Fairford, thirty-six Stirlings were prepared to tow gliders carrying troops to Normandy during the evening of D-Day.

The Fairford squadrons' next big operation came with the 17 September assault on Arnhem. Large numbers of Stirlings and Horsas were flown to Holland during the first two days with an enormous supply task to follow. During this attack a large number of aircraft were lost to enemy fighters and anti-aircraft fire. In October 1944 thirty-two Horsas were towed to Rome/Ciampino, of which twenty-seven arrived. The Stirlings left Fairford, and next to arrive were Albemarle towing aircraft and their US-built Hadrian gliders which belonged to No.22 Heavy Glider Conversion Unit. They stayed until October 1945. In early 1946 three flights of Oxford trainers were based at Fairford but in September four squadrons of Halifax four-engined aircraft flew in when the station became the principle airborne forces base in the UK. They remained here for two years. Fairford was without occupants for some three.

On 1 July 1951 Fairford became a US Air Force Strategic Air Command base with longer and stronger runways, and bigger accommodation for aircraft and personnel. It was not until 7 February 1953 that seventeen giant B-36 bombers flew in after a flight from Texas. Then, on 7 April two B-47 Stratojets arrived to lead a group of forty-five B-47s of 306th Bomb Wing. They returned home in September 1953. For most of the ensuing decade there was a constant rotation of B-36 and B-47 squadrons at Fairford.

In June 1964 Fairford was handed back to the RAF and became home to the scarlet Gnat trainers of the Red Arrows formation aerobatic team from early 1965 until September 1966. By then No.53 Squadron's Belfast transports were temporarily based at Fairford. In 1968 Nos 47 and 30 Squadrons moved in with their new Hercules transports flying troops and cargo overseas.

Because of its long runways and good facilities and its comparative proximity to Filton, from 1969 until 1977 Fairford became the base for test flying the British-built Concordes. The resident Hercules continued to operate here until February 1971. It was in September 1978 the US Air Force KC-135 tanker aircraft were stationed at Fairford for refuelling duties during NATO exercises. During the 1991 Gulf War and in the 2003 war against Iraq, US Air Force B-52 bombers operated from Fairford.

In 1985 the International Air Tattoo moved to Fairford where it set up its headquarters. From then until 1993, when a Russian Tupolev 95 'Bear' landed in Britain for the first time, the Tattoos were biennial; thereafter they became annual events, becoming the Royal International Air Tattoo in 1996, marking its 25th Anniversary. Europe's largest air show, with some 400 aircraft from over forty air arms taking part in 2002, it attracts 200,000 visitors, offering thirteen hours of entertainment on each of the two days. Above all the Tattoo is a major fund-raising event for the RAF Benevolent Fund.

Filton

4 miles N of Bristol

When the British & Colonial Aeroplane Co. was formed at Filton in 1910 it bought land to become an airfield. The Bristol Boxkite was the first of some 180 types and sub-types of aircraft test flown at Filton.

Apart from BCAC, Royal Flying Corps squadrons used Filton to exercise before going to France during the First World War. No.5 Aircraft Acceptance Park occupied eighteen hangars on the airfield and test flew new aircraft from the manufacturers before issuing them to squadrons. In 1923 the company, now named Bristol Aeroplane Co., was contracted to operate a Reserve Flying School. Six years later No.501 (County of Gloucester) Squadron was formed at Filton flying Avro 504N trainers, later using DH 9A operational aircraft. This Reserve squadron became an operational RAF unit in September 1939 flying Hurricanes, and moved from Filton. It was replaced by the Gladiators of No.263 Squadron which took part in an ill-fated Norwegian campaign in April 1940. Other squadrons moved in for short periods for the defence of Bristol and the West Country and then, in April 1941, No.263 returned with Whirlwind fighters. These were flown on convoy patrol duties and in low-level attacks on targets in France. Although this was the last operational squadron to be based at Filton a Ferry Flight and an Overseas Aircraft Preparation Unit moved in. In 1943 the US Army Air Force set up a Mobile Repair and Reclamation Squadron which remained at Filton until June 1944.

Post-war, the main runway was lengthened to enable Bristol's big Brabazon airliner to be flight tested at Filton, No.501 Squadron reformed as an Auxiliary Air Force unit in May 1946, Bristol University Air Squadron was activated and a Reserve Flying School was based there. With the general reduction of reserve forces, in 1953 the school disbanded, to be followed four years later by No.501 Squadron. In 2003 Filton is still home to the Bristol UAS and an Air Experience Flight which provides this service to Air Training Corps and Combined Cadet Force cadets. Airbus UK, the current name of the company at Filton and Rolls-Royce use the airfield for a number of flying duties.

No.19 Squadron, Royal Flying Corps was stationed at Filton between 4 April and 10 July 1916 when it moved to St Omer, France. Here, squadron ground crew gather round a very dishevelled RE.8 scout in 1917.

Formed in March 1965 at RAF Fairford, the Red Arrows, seen flying British Aerospace Hawks, moved to Kemble in August 1966 and went to Scampton in November 1986.

Kemble

4 miles SW of Cirencester

Apart from being an important railway station on the Gloucester – London line, Kemble is home to an RAF airfield which served as an aircraft store throughout its Service life. The first occupant in June 1938 was No.5 Maintenance Unit and by the end of 1939 some 500 aircraft were 'in the stores', numbers of them in the open. When a lone Junkers 88 strayed into the county in July 1940 a Hurricane of Kemble's Defence Flight shot it down – then crashed, killing its pilot, Pilot Officer Bird. An Air Delivery Flight began work in January 1941 but many aircraft were dispersed to Satellite Landing Grounds. During 1942 large numbers of Hurricanes, Typhoons, Albemarles and Lancasters were delivered and over 500 Wellingtons were sent to the Middle East. New runways and taxiways were built during 1943.

In the preparations for the 1944 Normandy landings the emphasis was turned to Typhoons which were needed in large numbers and later transport aircraft for use overseas. By December 1945 the total aircraft held by the MU peaked at over 1,000, and in 1952 nearly 600 Sabre jet fighters flew in from Canada to be given a camouflage paint scheme. It was then the turn of the RAF's Hunters at Kemble to arrive in 1954 for modernisation. In the following year Gnat jet trainers from the Central Flying School at Little Rissington operated from Kemble. While CFS scarlet-painted Gnats at Kemble were flown by its aerobatic team under the name of the 'Red Arrows', it was not until later that they became the RAF's official formation aerobatic team. While at Kemble in 1980 the 'Reds' changed their Gnats for the bigger Hawk aircraft and when they left Kemble it became the US Air Force's Support Centre Europe, yet another storage unit.

In 1995 Kemble Flying Club was formed and not only launched the airfield into civil aviation but undertook its early development with much success. Soon afterwards Delta Jets moved in operating Hunters, Gnats and Jet Provost aircraft owned by syndicates. It trains suitably qualified pilots to fly these aircraft and provides engineering support for them. BCT Aviation Kemble was formed in 2002 as a flying school with one aircraft but rapidly had a growing fleet for trainee pilots. Originally named Mason Air another Kemble-based unit is Aero School Kemble which provides tuition and aircraft hire facilities. In 1996 the Bristol Aero Collection moved to Kemble from Banwell, Weston-super-Mare, bringing a Britannia, 1919 Babe biplane, scale example of a Boxkite, two helicopters and a great range of engines and missiles.

Leighterton

3 miles SW of Tetbury

This airfield opened early in 1918, the first unit based there being Nos 7 and 8 (Training) Squadron, Australian Flying Corps flying Avro 504s and RE.8s. A year later they were succeeded by two RAF squadrons. Between the wars this airfield became a private aerodrome but in 1940 it was turned into a decoy site for RAF Hullavington, being bombed on several occasions. It was later returned to agricultural use when they were disbanded at the end of the war, the buildngs were sold and dismantled with some being re-built on local sites as barns and village halls.

Little Rissington

4 miles S of Stow-on-the-Wold

It opened in August 1938 and throughout its life 'Rissi' was used by pilot-flying training units and was home to No.8 MU. The first aircraft on this station were Fury fighters and twin-engined Ansons followed by US-built Harvards. But soon Wellington bombers and Spitfires arrived at the MU which, by 1940 had over 400 aircraft in store with a single

Provost side-by-side ab initio trainers were flown by Little Rissington's Central Flying School Basic Flight in 1952.

Spitfire on stand-by for local defence in the event of air attack. When the MU's hangars overflowed aircraft were dispersed to a number of nearby airfields. Several Reserve Landing Grounds at Kemble, Chipping Norton and Middle Farm were used and in October 1941 a Blind Approach Training Flight for night and bad-weather training was formed and operated at 'Rissi' until the end of the war. No.6 Pilots Advanced Flying Unit had some 120 twin-engined Oxford and Anson trainers on its strength by 1942 and the MU was assembling Horsa and Hotspur gliders, and pre-war biplanes were being refurbished as glider-tugs. In 1945 nearly 1,400 aircraft were held by the MU there and at two other locations. When training stopped in November 1945 no less than 5,400 pilots had been trained at Rissington and they had received over 700 gallantry awards including four Victoria Crosses.

The Central Flying School, which trained pilots to be instructors, was based at this airfield in 1946 with the ubiquitous Tiger Moths. During the ensuing thirty years more advanced aircraft were used: Chipmunks, Provosts, Jet Provosts, Vampires and Meteors. In April 1976 the school left Little Rissington which closed in August when the Army moved in. Later it was occupied by a US hospital.

Long Newnton

3 miles NW of Malmesbury

Originally a 'Q Site' or decoy airfield for Kemble, Long Newnton was taken over by two Service Flying Training Schools in 1941 and later became a satellite airfield for a Flying Unit at South Cerney. At the war's end it became a storage unit and finally closed in about 1949 and became agricultural land.

Moreton-in-Marsh

Two miles E of Moreton-in-Marsh

This airfield will always be associated with the Wellington twin-engined bombers (known as 'the cloth bomber' because of its fabric covering) based there for most of the war. No.21 Operational Training Unit began flying in March 1941 training Wellington crews by dropping leaflets in France, but by the end of the year the emphasis was on training solely for Wellingtons operating in the Middle East. Delivering these aircraft involved long-distance ferry flights which, to avoid enemy aircraft, were routed out over the Atlantic then down to Gibraltar and onwards, and a Ferry Training Flight was activated at Moreton. In addition, operational flights were made carrying bombs or leaflets, and night exercises over the UK were routine. Operational flying stopped in mid-1944, other training units and aircraft arrived and departed, and the RAF finally left in 1959. Moreton-in-Marsh was then used for Fire Service training and in July 1981 the Fire Service College was established there. A small museum in the town commemorates the Wellington.

Moreton Valence

4 miles S of Gloucester

This airfield opened in November 1939 named Haresfield and was used by Ansons from Staverton's Air Observer Navigation School; two years later it became Moreton Valence. Then, in October 1943, Gloster Aircraft Co. established its production and experimental flight-test and service departments there for Meteor jet aircraft as the main Brockworth airfield and factory were not so suitable. Other training units moved in but the RAF left this airfield in October 1946. Gloster carried out test flying on Meteors and Javelins at 'MV' until July 1962 when the airfield closed. Today the M5 motorway sits on top of the old main runway.

Northleach

10 miles NE of Cirencester

Used for training by Hotspur gliders and Master tugs from Stoke Orchard, Northleach opened in November 1942 but its exposed location on the Cotswolds caused flying to be intermittent and subject to the weather. Thus, it was abandoned in late 1944.

Moreton Valence airfield 1952, with Gloster Aircraft's Service, Flight Test and Development buildings. Beyond, the Severn loops its way seawards.

North Stoke

4 miles NW of Bath

Located high on Lansdown Racecourse from mid-1943, Oxfords of Nos 3 and 7 Flying Instructors Schools used this Relief Landing Ground having flown over from their Castle Coombe base each day for 'circuits-and-bumps'. This ended in July 1944.

Overley

5 miles NW of Cirencester

Opened in January 1942 as a Satellite Landing Ground where dispersed aircraft could be stored, a runway and hard-standings were built and aircraft, some of them big four-engined types, were soon being parked in the open. Other flying units also used it for practice landings. All this activity stopped in October 1945 and the airfield was vacated.

Rendcombe

5 miles N of Cirencester

Opening in early 1916 No.48 Squadron Royal Flying Corps began flying BE.12s and Bristol F.2b Fighters here between June 1916 and early 1917. The fighters then moved to France. A Reserve Squadron formed at Rendcomb and became a Training Squadron with Fighters and No.62 Squadron's Fighters worked up before flying to France in January 1918. By then No.110 Squadron with BE.2cs had arrived and left after two weeks there. For different periods Rendcomb then became home to five training and operational squadrons flying various aircraft, including DH.6s and RE.8s before flying ceased in late 1919. In 1991 Vic Norman bought the site and developed it to create an airfield to rekindle the spirit and panache of those early flying days. Currently Aerosuperbatics, an aerobatic display team headed by Vic, is based at Rendcomb flying 1940s Boeing Stearman Kaydet biplanes modified for 'wing-walking' by glamorous – and brave – girls.

South Cerney

3 miles SE of Cirencester

Throughout its long RAF life South Cerney was home to flying and administration training Schools. It opened in August 1937 with Audax trainer aircraft of No.3 Service Flying Training School; also it was the first to fly the twin-engined Oxford trainers which arrived in mid-1938. The airfield was bombed on three occasions with only minimal damage.

Handley Page Hampden bombers were among the heavier aircraft stored by No.20 MU at Overley in 1942. These carry No.185 Squadron code letters GL-T.

Three Blind Approach Training Flights moved in and out during 1943–45. Post-war, the Flying Training Command Instructors' School was at South Cerney for a few months, leaving in February 1947 and a year later the Tiger Moths of No.2 Flying Training School arrived. In August 1954 the RAF's first helicopter instructors training unit was formed as the Central Flying School (Helicopter Squadron), flying Dragonflies, Sycamores and Whirlwinds. Two more Training Schools resided here until January 1968 when it was taken over by RAF Air Support Command. Finally, it became British Army property and was renamed Duke of Gloucester Barracks.

Southrop

2 miles NE of Fairford

First used in August 1940 by No.2 Flying Training School, this Relief Landing Ground was a grass strip with two runways. Two Pilots' Advanced Flying Units used it in succession until January 1945. It was closed during that year.

Staverton

3 miles NE of Gloucester

Originally a small grass strip activated by the Cotswold Aero Club in September 1932, when plans for a Gloucester and Cheltenham Airport were being formulated it was decided to buy land on the north side of the old A40 road opposite to the club's site. Work on the airport began in November 1934 and it was licenced two years later with Railway Air Services flying in on its Bristol-Birmingham route.

In 1937, when the RAF Expansion Schemes were well underway, the Air Ministry was given use of the airfield in return for making improvements and installing new equipment. No.31 Elementary and Reserve Flying Training School formed in September 1938

Serialled P1775, this Folland 43/37 flying engine test-bed, the 'Folland Frightful', with a Bristol Centaurus engine, seen at RAF Staverton in March 1942.

operating Tiger Moths. Next year a Civil School of Air Navigation moved in with DH Dragon Rapides. Rotol Airscrews, whose factory was near the original grass strip, set up its Flight Test Department on the airfield. There followed several name changes for the training schools and in September 1939 the airport became RAF Staverton. The following year the ubiquitous Ansons arrived for the Navigation School and Tiger Moths for No.2 EFTS. Another industrial unit to join Staverton was Folland Aircraft's flight test section which was working on several of its 43/37 flying engine test-bed aircraft. It was known universally as the 'Folland Frightful', a name given to it by Gloster test pilot Neil 'Mike' Daunt after one broke-up in mid-air when he was testing it. Then Gloster Aircraft began flying Hurricanes from Staverton in 1941 while a runway was being put down at Brockworth. Flight Refuelling arrived in 1942 to carry out development of its in-flight refuelling systems, plus other research work including towing fighter aircraft with Wellington bombers. In December the Advanced Flying Unit departed leaving the three industrial companies as the main users of the airfield. By 1946 all Service flying had ceased but two years later the RAF Police Dog Training School and No.1 RAF Police Wing were based there.

The Air Ministry relinquished occupancy of Staverton in September 1950 leaving it without any controlling organisation. Cambrian Airways managed it for three years from March 1953 but eventually pulled out leaving Smiths Development Flight, which had moved in during that year too, to assume management responsibility for this airfield. This was handed over to the Gloucester and Cheltenham councils in 1962. During the following few years Glosair was formed to provide aircraft-servicing facilities and assemble Australian Victa Airtourer light aeroplanes, the Skyfame Museum was opened and Derby Airways, to be followed by Intra, operated DC-3s and Viscounts on summer services. Staverton, now Gloucestershire Airport, following a multi-million pound investment, has a new terminal building, flying control services and equipment. It is home to three flying schools, a similar number of maintenance organisations and houses some 100 light aircraft and business jets.

Stoke Orchard

2 miles W of Bishop's Cleeve

Located at the southern end of the Vale of Evesham, small wonder this airfield has the word 'orchard' in its name. The Tiger Moths of No.10 Elementary Flying Training School (EFTS) arrived on 23 September 1941 and shared the airfield with Gloster Aircraft's dispersed Hurricane wing assembly shop and flight shed. When the school closed in July 1942 No.3 Glider Training School was formed with Master towing aircraft and Hotspur glider trainers. A GAC employee's parked car was written off when a towing bridle, jettisoned by a Master, slashed down on it. To relieve the pressure on the local airspace some training was moved to other airfields. Flying continued at Stoke Orchard until January 1945 and the airfield was vacated later that year.

General Aircraft Hotspur gliders of No.3 Glider Training School at RAF Stoke Orchard land in formation in 1943.

Windrush

4 miles W of Burford

In early summer 1940 this grass Relief Landing Ground welcomed No.6 Service Flying Training School which operated day and night training. Very soon it was to witness a heroic act of self-sacrifice. When a lone Heinkel 111 bomber dropped bombs close to the airfield during the evening of 18 August, its crew spotted an RAF Anson twin-engined trainer directly ahead of them, its navigation lights shining in the dusk. They then opened fire on the Anson. Its pilot, Sergeant Bruce Hancock, immediately switched off his lights. Eye witnesses reported that Hancock then banked to port and deliberately pulled up directly into the path of the Heinkel, smashing into it. Sgt Hancock and the crew of the enemy aircraft were killed as the wreckage fell in flames. As if in retribution for the loss of their bomber the Luftwaffe twice attacked Windrush the following month, but their bombs fell well away from the airfield. Oxfords from Little Rissington used Windrush during 1941 and by the following year two runways with Sommerfield Tracking had been laid. Flying training continued virtually until this airfield closed in 1945.

Yate

10 miles NE of Bristol

This airfield was built during 1917 and No.3 (Western) Aircraft Repair Depot was formed there on 12 October that year with some large sheds and workshops. The depot was disbanded in May 1920 and the airfield was abandoned. Five years later George Parnall & Co. acquired it for production of the aircraft of its own design and of other companies. In 1935 this company was taken over by Nash & Thompson Ltd and was renamed Parnall Aircraft Ltd. Its wartime production was powered gun turrets of Nash & Thompson design plus Spitfire, Lancaster and Lincoln sub-assemblies. This factory was bombed by the Luftwaffe on three occasions, a main railway line which ran past it being a too readily identified pointer to the site. In January 1944 No.92 Gliding School opened at Yate but moved out when the airfield closed the following year and was built over.

Gliding Sites & Clubs

There are two main gliding sites in Gloucestershire; the Bristol and Gloucestershire Gliding Club at Nympsfield and the Cotswold Gliding Club at Aston Down. The Bristol and Gloucestershire Club was formed in 1938 at Leighterton, near Tetbury, but the Second World War stopped all civil gliding activities. The club was resurrected in 1946 with members being drawn principally from Bristol Aeroplane Co. Leighterton was not an ideal site and a hill-site was sought. Meanwhile flying continued at Lulsgate Bottom, an ex-RAF airfield and now Bristol Airport, where, in September 1946 the club's Kirby Cadet was the first regular post-war aeroplane to use that airfield. In 1956 the club moved to its present site at Nympsfield.

The Cotswold Gliding Club was formed at Long Newnton in August 1964 and moved to Aston Down three years later. Since then it has acquired large areas of the airfield inside the perimeter track, has two large hangars and has erected other administrative and domestic buildings. Over the years it has hosted National and Regional Gliding Championships, including Junior Championships at its splendid Aston Down site. In addition to sharing Gloucestershire airspace with Nympsfield's gliders the Cotswold Club's members have made many long-range flights to North Wales and Scotland.

Postscript

If one had to choose Gloucestershire's major aviation achievement, what would it be? Certainly the incredible out-pouring of aeroplanes plus the men to fly them in two World Wars; perhaps the sleeve-valve radial engines, the Olympus turbofan and Pegasus vectored thrust engines or Britain's first jet fighter; then there are the composite-bladed propeller, the development of the electric auto-pilot, automatic-landing systems and glass cockpits; not to forget the internally-sprung wheel and the liquid-spring shock-absorber. The choice is yours. There is no doubt about the most historic and prophetic piece of paper. It was the one carrying the eight words which Gloster Aircraft Co.'s test pilot, Gerry Sayer, wrote on his report sheet after the first flight of Britain's and the Allies' first experimental jet aircraft, the Gloster E.28/39. After listing the type of landing gear, the quantities of oil and fuel carried and the tyre pressures, he came to a section marked 'Propeller Type'. Gerry could have just put a line through it. But he paused....then wrote 'No propeller needed for this type of propulsion'. Aviation had changed forever.

Right: *Gerry Sayer, Gloster Aircraft Co.'s test pilot, who first flew the Gloster E.28/39, Britain's and the Allies' first jet aircraft, on 15 May 1941.*

Opposite
A typed and signed copy of Gerry Sayers' test report after the first flight of the Gloster E.28/39.

A

GLOSTER AIRCRAFT CO. LTD.

TEST FLIGHT REPORT No. : 1

PILOT P.E.G.Sayer.

Type of Test : 1st Flight. General experience of the type.

Date and Time of Start 15.5.41. 1940 hrs. Duration 17 mins.

AIRCRAFT : Type and No. E.28/39. W.4041.

Type of Undercarriage Dowty nose wheel type. All retractable.

Other Features Main wheel lever suspension type. Nose wheel strut type.

AIRSCREW : Type and No. No airscrew fitted with this method of propulsion.

Dia. :

Pitch Setting Fine .... Coarse

Ground Clearance Flying Position .... Tail on Ground

ENGINE : Type and No. Whittle Supercharger Type W.1.

Reduction Gear

R.P.M. O.G. Fine Pitch 16500 Take-off. Coarse Pitch

Boost O.G. " " " "

Type of Air Intake

Radiator Stbd radiator blanked off. Port radiator in circuit.

Other Features

WEIGHTS CARRIED : Petrol Paraffin 50 galls. Oil 1 gall.

Cooling Liquid 3.5 galls water.

Total Weight 3441 lb. estimated from Test C.G.

C.G. Position .284 A.M.C. U/C Down. .297 A.M.C. U/C Up calculated from (Tare C.G.

Loading Sht. No. 142 Date 7.5.41.

REMARKS :

Exhaust System

Cooling System

Oil System

Guns and Mountings

Bombs and Racks

Sights

Nav. and Ident. Lamps

Aerial

Fairing

Type of Cockpit Heating

Pilot Position & Type

Nose wheel leg total travel 12" as against 10" on original nose wheel leg fitted for taxying trials at Brockworth. Static travel 6" instead of 7" on the first leg. Nose wheel strut pressure reduced from 140 lbsq.in. to 115 lbsq.in. Tyre pressure reduced from 35 lbsq.in. to 20 lbsq.in. Steering on nose wheel 11° either side of the centre line Brakes on all three wheels.

TEST INSTRUMENTS :

Ican. Altimeter No. : .... Calibrated

A.S.I. Instrument No. : .... "

R.P.M. " " .... "

Boost Gauge .. " .... "

Air Temp. .. " ....

Signature of Pilot

Other local titles published by Tempus

Bristol Aeroplane Company A History

DEREK N. JAMES

This great aviation company has occupied premises at Filton for ninety years, employing thousands of skilful hands and agile innovative brains to create flying machines: from stick and string, wood and canvas to stainless steel, titanium and composites; from fixed-wing triplanes to rotary-wings; from fighters, bombers, and transports to supersonic airliners, missiles and spacecraft.

0 7524 1754 1

Gloster Aircraft Company

DEREK N. JAMES

It is difficult to imagine that the parishes of Hucclecote and Brockworth were once home to one of Britain's major aircraft manufacturers.

Gloster Aircraft Company produced some 10,000 aeroplanes and provided employment for countless thousands of local people. They designed some outstanding fighter aircraft and designed and built Britain's first jet aircraft.

0 7524 0038 X

Filton Voices

JANE TOZER AND JACKIE SIMS

This book was compiled by Jane Tozer and Jackie Sims for the Filton Community History Project. The many fascinating stories are complemented by a hundred photographs drawn from the private collections of the contributors. Community history at its best!

0 7524 3097 1

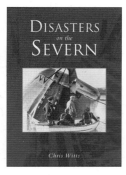

Disasters on the Severn

CHRIS WITTS

In Disasters on the Severn, Chris Witts, an experienced navigator of the river, has compiled a fascinating catalogue of such incidents. As well as recounting historical crises, he also tells of his personal experiences of difficulty, panic and loss on the river.

0 7524 2383 5

To discover more Tempus titles please visit us at:
www.tempus-publishing.com